Jane Austen

Jane Austen

*An
Unrequited
Love*

ANDREW NORMAN

Love, they say, is like a Rose;
I'm sure 'tis like the wind that blows,
For not a human creature knows
How it comes or where it goes.

Miss Austen (Jane)

First published 2009
This edition published 2010

The History Press
The Mill, Brimscombe Port
Stroud, Gloucestershire, GL5 2QG
www.thehistorypress.co.uk

© Andrew Norman, 2009, 2010

The right of Andrew Norman to be identified as the Author
of this work has been asserted in accordance with the
Copyrights, Designs and Patents Act 1988.

British Library Cataloguing in Publication Data.
A catalogue record for this book is available from the British Library.

ISBN 978 0 7524 5529 7

Typesetting and origination by The History Press
Printed in Great Britain

Contents

Foreword

Dr Norman has written an excellent biography of Jane Austen, which I have thoroughly enjoyed reading. He has kept my interest throughout with his easy style and, having written it from a doctor's point of view, has noticed entirely different aspects of her life and times from those which we are used to reading about in her letters, novels etc. This makes it of great interest to us all, especially as he progresses through her family. In particular, he describes how Jane's own health, or latterly her lack of good health, affected her writing, especially the fragment of *Sanditon* written in 1817 when her youth and bloom had faded. This was a novel in the making in a style entirely different to her normal one. What a very great pity she was not well enough to complete it. Dr Norman has also drawn attention to the influence which Jane's exotic cousin Eliza, Comtesse de Feuillide had, both on Jane as a person, and as a writer.

I think that Dr Norman probably asked me to write the foreword to his book because he had heard that I was closely related to Jane Austen and have studied her work, life and times for very many years. Both my grandmothers, Elizabeth ('Lizzie') Bradford (*née* Knight) and Louisa Hardy (*née* Knight) – who were sisters – were granddaughters of Jane Austen's very wealthy and generous brother Edward Knight (formerly Austen) with whom both Jane and her sister Cassandra often spent months at a time.

It was Edward who gave Mrs Austen, Cassandra and Jane the Chawton Cottage in which they could live comfortably. This was situated near to Edward's own Chawton House – or 'The Great House' as they always knew it – built in Elizabethan times by John Knight. My father, Edward Austen Bradford, was brought up there (having a wet-nurse in the village when a baby while his mother Lizzie had to go back to India to my Grandpapa: her husband, Indian Army officer, Sir Edward Bradford). Also, my father married from 'The Great House', as did both my grandmothers.

Dr Norman deduces from her writing that Jane Austen was fiercely egalitarian, feeling very strongly that men, and women too, should be judged on their merits of character, judgement and education rather than their connections or their bank balance. Jane Austen was the first novelist to expect women to have the same moral values and standards as men, and this is one of the reasons that her novels are as relevant today as when they were first written.

There is a deep underlying humanity in all of Jane's novels and one can sense that courage and humanity were very much part of her make-up. She demonstrates that young people are often very bad judges of what will make them happy. However, if a character in her novels is found wanting, she does not seek to destroy them or humiliate them. This is an Austen trait. Peaceful co-existence is the order of the day, as Jane's naval brothers discovered when they came to stay. There were never disagreements as it was not their habit (neither is it the habit of the family today).

Jane showed that she was very much aware of the disadvantages suffered by young women entering the job market due to a lack of education and also a lack of available paid work for women. She also wanted to warn them not to rush into a relationship without due consideration, in case they were abandoned and left with a babe.

Luckily, Jane's ability to see the humorous side of things permits the present-day reader to look back at her life and times, and the lives of her contemporaries, in the same light-hearted way, rather than judging them by present-day standards.

Doctor Norman's book is a pleasure to read and you will be rewarded with information of great interest!

Diana Shervington, July 2008
A Vice-President of the Jane Austen Society

Preface

Whereas many aspects of Jane Austen's life are well known and well documented, others are shrouded in mystery. This was not as a result of any action on her part; it was principally because of the actions of her sister Cassandra.

Jane Austen scholar Deirdre Le Faye, for example, in her book *Jane Austen's Letters*, has demonstrated that numerous letters – sent by Jane to family and friends – are missing from the years 1796, 1798–1801, 1805, 1807–09 and 1811–15. (That these letters once existed can be deduced from the contents of the ones which survive.) In particular, no letters whatsoever survive for the period between June 1801 to September 1804. Also, Edward, Lord Brabourne – Jane's great-nephew – refers to 'nearly two letterless years' between 6 June 1811 and 24 May 1813[1]. What is the explanation for this? If a recipient saved *some* of Jane's letters then why not all of them?

The answer is provided by Jane's niece Caroline, daughter of her eldest brother James, who states, with reference to these missing letters:

> My Aunt [Cassandra] looked them over and burnt the greater part, (as she told me), two or three years before her own death – She left, or gave some as legacies to the Neices [*sic*] – but of those that I have seen, several had portions cut out.[2]

What prompted Cassandra to act in this way? Author Constance Hill refers to an article by Jane's niece Anna Lefroy (*née* Austen), 'that appeared in Temple Bar some years ago'. In it Anna, referring to the missing letters, declares that Jane:

> . . . was a woman most reticent as to her own deepest and holiest feelings; and her sister Cassandra would have thought she was sinning against that delicacy and reserve had she left behind her any record of them . . .[3]

Deirdre Le Faye took the view that Cassandra decided to destroy many of the letters:

> . . . because Jane had either described [her own] physical symptoms rather too fully, or else because she had made some comment about other members of the family which Cassandra did not wish posterity to read about.[4]

Granted, this may certainly have been the case with many of the destroyed letters. However, it should be pointed out that Cassandra made no effort to destroy those in which Jane referred to her short and painful relationship with Tom Lefroy; or those in which Jane described, in detail, the symptoms of the disease which would finally terminate her life.

So could Cassandra have had another, quite different motive? Was there a more profound reason for her act of destruction; one which had nothing whatsoever to do with Jane's alleged sensibilities? Was it Cassandra's view that if these letters were to be made public then the relationship between herself and her sister – hitherto portrayed as loving and idyllic – would be seen in a somewhat different light?

Acknowledgements

I am grateful to the following for their help:

Chawton House Library, Chawton; Devon Record Office, Exeter; Exeter Local Studies Library; Hampshire Record Office; Jane Austen's House and Museum Collections; Plymouth Central Library; Sidmouth Parish Church; Westcountry Studies Library, Exeter; Lyme Regis Museum. Also to the Brotherton Library, University of Leeds; Emmanuel College Cambridge Archives; Society of Genealogists; Victoria & Albert Museum.

And to Tibbie Adams; Ronald Bragg; Max Hebditch; Joan Jordan.

I am especially grateful to Diana Shervington and, as always, to my dear wife Rachel for all her help and encouragement.

Introduction

The small village of Steventon near Basingstoke in Hampshire would probably have remained largely unknown to the world had it not been for the fact that there, on 16 December 1775, Jane Austen was born. It is also true to say that were it not for her six completed novels, poems, and several other minor works and uncompleted fragments, our knowledge of country life during that period would be that much the poorer.

Jane's novels, in the main, share a common theme: the necessity for a young lady – the heroine – to find a man of sufficient wealth and income, perhaps £10,000 a year, in order that she might marry and live in circumstances to which she is, or would like to become accustomed. Yet it is not quite as simple as that; for the prospective partner will be no good unless he or she possesses certain qualities to be admired.

In the vicinity of Steventon were many stately homes occupied by the landed nobility and gentry, where Jane attended balls and social functions. Her letters reveal just how much she enjoyed this aspect of her life. She describes what she proposes to wear at such occasions and afterwards, describes in equal detail who was there. More interestingly, she gives her opinion as to the qualities of certain individuals and his or her suitability as a prospective partner. The question is, would Jane herself, the author whose fictional characters with their lives and loves are today well known throughout the world, find love in her own life?

❧ 1 ❧

Steventon:
The Cradle of Jane's Genius

Steventon in Hampshire, the birthplace of English novelist Jane Austen, was said by William Austen-Leigh, Jane's great-nephew and grandson of her eldest brother James, to be 'the cradle of her genius'.

The hamlet, with its cottages, church, rectory, and manor house, was situated 6 miles from Basingstoke amidst rolling hills, woodland and farmland. A drawing by Jane's niece Anna Lefroy, daughter of her eldest brother James, depicts Steventon in the late eighteenth century. Here, in a meandering leafy lane, are sturdy-looking cottages with climbing plants ascending their walls and hurdle fencing and wicket gates enclosing their gardens. And who inhabited these cottages? Why, shepherds and farm labourers whose wives and children assisted them in the fields, especially at harvest time.

In the words of Oxford scholar R.W. Chapman:

> The north Hampshire chalk is a thin soil and does not grow the finest trees. But it is a country of pleasing irregularities, abounding in lanes and lovely farms and cottages.[1]

James E. Austen-Leigh, son of Jane's brother James, describes how, in the shelter of Steventon's hedgerows, primroses, anemones and wild hyacinths grew. Whereas in the churchyard were to be found sweet violets, both purple and white, 'which grew, "in abundance" beneath the church's south wall'. Here, also, were to be found 'large elms . . . old hawthorns', and 'the hollow yew tree'.[2]

As for the surrounding area, small thickets or plantations of trees dotted the landscape – Burnt Wood, Popham Woods and Nutley Wood, for example. But generally, this was a landscape of fields devoted to crop-growing and cattle- and sheep-grazing. (In former times there were areas of common land, such as Basingstoke Down and Basingstoke Fields to the east, where the lower classes had been accustomed to graze their animals or collect acorns for their pigs to eat, or timber and turf for firewood. This land had, however, been swallowed up by the Enclosure Acts of 1787 and transferred to private ownership.) At nearby Overton there were silk mills and a brickworks.

Although not located on a main thoroughfare, the hamlet of Steventon was by no means cut off – except perhaps in winter when deep snow lay on the ground. A mile or so to the north was the Basingstoke to Andover road from where it was possible to catch the London coach, two of which ran nightly, from Dean Gate. On this road lay Overton – the post-town – which was where a main branch of the Post Office was situated. Likewise, a mile or so to the south was the Basingstoke to Winchester road, known as Popham Lane, along which coaches also ran.[3]

Steventon is recorded as a manor (feudal lordship) in the *Domesday Book* – a comprehensive record of the extent, value and ownership of the land made in 1086 by order of King William I. However, there is no mention of a church there, although churches were recorded at the nearby villages of Ashe and Deane. Nonetheless, evidence that the Saxons may have worshipped there is provided by the limestone fragment of the shaft of a Saxon cross, believed to date from the ninth century, which was discovered in 1877. It had been used in the construction of one of the walls of Steventon Manor House.

The Norman Church of St Nicholas, Steventon, with its crenulated tower and spire, was built in about the year 1200 by the lords of the manor: the de Luvers family; minor alterations were made in the thirteenth, fifteenth and nineteenth centuries. The stencilled wall paintings which decorate the chancel arch are thought to date from the Victorian era, whereas the small decorated area below the wall light to the right of the chancel arch is from the medieval period.

Here, members of the Austen family served as clergymen from 1754–1873, a period of 119 years. They were curate Thomas Bathurst (1754–65), and rectors Henry Austen (1759–61), George Austen (1761–1805), James Austen (1805–19), Henry Thomas Austen (1820–23) and William Knight (1823–73). This is where Jane and four of her siblings: Henry, Cassandra, Francis and Charles, were baptised and where Jane's maternal grandmother Jane Leigh is buried.

When the Reverend George Austen arrived in Steventon in the spring of 1764, he found the church roof to be in a poor state of repair; the reason being that the spire, a pyramidal wooden structure atop the church tower, had blown down onto the roof in the winter of 1763–4 in a severe gale.

Steventon's Tudor manor house, with its 'circling screen of sycamores',[4] was situated adjacent to the church at the end of Church Walk. It was built by Sir Richard Pexall to replace the former Norman building which he demolished in 1560. The present occupants were the Digweeds who rented the property from the Knights of Godmersham Park, Kent.

Curiously, there were no cottages in the vicinity of the church and manor house, perhaps because the original hamlet had been destroyed by a pandemic of bubonic plague, known as the Black Death, which occurred in the fourteenth century.

✿ 2 ✿

Jane's Parents:
Steventon Rectory

Jane's father, the Revd George Austen, born in 1731, had an unpropitious beginning to his life. His mother Rebecca had died in 1732 when he was only a year old, whereupon his father William, a surgeon of Tonbridge, Kent, was subsequently remarried in 1736 to Susanna Kelk. When William died the following year at the early age of 36, Susanna promptly expelled George and his sisters, Philadelphia and Leonora, from the house. The children were sent to London to be looked after by their Uncle Stephen who was a bookseller. George was fortunate, however, in having another uncle – the wealthy Francis Austen of Sevenoaks – to pay for him to be educated at Tonbridge School and St John's College, Oxford, where he became a distinguished scholar and a Fellow from 1751–60. Meanwhile, in 1754 he was ordained. He then returned to his old school at Tonbridge as second master.

In 1761 George Austen became Rector of Steventon, Hampshire: a living presented to him by his kinsman Thomas Knight (I) of Godmersham Park, Kent. He remained non-resident and continued to live in Oxford where he was a don at St John's College; the parish was left to the care of his cousin the Revd Thomas Bathurst.

In his book *Jane Austen: Her Life and Letters*, William Austen-Leigh states that:

George Austen's handsome, placid, dignified features were an index to his mind. Serene in temper, devoted to his religion

and his family, a good father and a good scholar, he deserved
the love and respect which every evidence that we have shows
him to have gained from his family and his neighbours.[1]

Jane's mother was Cassandra, *née* Leigh, born in 1739, whose
family seat was Stoneleigh Abbey in Warwickshire. Cassandra
was proud of her Leigh family history, one of her ancestors
being Sir Thomas Leigh, who was Lord Mayor of London in
the reign of Queen Elizabeth I and who had ridden at the head
of the procession during the Queen's proclamation at St Paul's
Cathedral. In social terms, therefore, the Revd George Austen
had married somewhat above his station. Intellectually, however,
as a classical scholar, he was by no means Cassandra's inferior.

In his book *A Memoir of Jane Austen*, James E. Austen-Leigh
writes:

> In Mrs Austen . . . was to be found the germ of much of the
> ability which was concentrated in Jane, but of which others of
> her children had a share. She united strong common sense with
> a lively imagination, and often expressed herself, both in writ-
> ing and in conversation, with epigrammatic force and point.[2]

James E. Austen-Leigh might also have mentioned that Mrs
Austen was an expert at needlework and 'wrote in an admi-
rable hand, both powerful and interesting'.[3] Her talent for
writing poetry was recognised at the age of 6 when her uncle,
Theophilus Leigh, Master of Balliol College, Oxford, described
her as 'already the poet of the family'.

When the Revd George Austen married Cassandra Leigh
on 26 April 1764, the newly-weds immediately moved to
Hampshire and took up residence, not at Steventon, but at the
rectory at Deane. This was because Steventon Rectory – invariably referred to as The Parsonage – suffered from damp and

was in a state of disrepair. This is not surprising, as the rectory was situated in a valley into which the fields of the glebe lands (lands attached to the parish church), including 'Quintence Meadow', 'South Meadow', 'Home Meadow', 'East Meadow', 'Nursery Meadow' and 'Hanging Meadow', all drained. (Only a fraction of this land was occupied by the Revd Austen, as will be seen.) In the words of William Austen-Leigh:

> The rectory had been of the most miserable description but George Austen improved it until it became a tolerably roomy and convenient habitation.[4]

Rent was payable by the Austens to the Rector of Deane, the Revd William Hillman, who, having private means, chose to live at nearby Ashe Park rather than at the rectory. R.W. Chapman stated that the Revd Austen 'improved and enlarged [Steventon Rectory] until it was sufficiently commodious to hold pupils [of his] in addition to a growing family'.[5]

Steventon Rectory was situated on the south side of the Steventon to North Waltham road, near to the corner of Church Walk which led to the Parish Church of St Nicholas, a quarter of a mile away. A woodcut depicting the front of the rectory, which appeared in James E. Austen-Leigh's *A Memoir of Jane Austen*, published in 1870, shows it to be a substantial property, even before it was enlarged. As for the Revd Austen's alterations, they are evident from an illustration of the rear of the rectory – executed by Anna Lefroy – where it is apparent that two substantial two-storey wings have been added, one at either side.

These works took several years to accomplish and it was not until about 1768 that the Austens were able to transfer to Steventon Rectory. In that year, Susanna (*née* Kelk), the Revd Austen's widowed stepmother, who had expelled George and his sisters from the family home, died, whereupon George received the sum of about £1,200 from the sale of the family house. Likewise, when Mrs Austen's mother Jane (*née* Walker), widow of the Revd Thomas Leigh, died – also in the same year – the former received a legacy of some £1,000.

R. W. Chapman's work entitled *Jane Austen: Facts and Problems* contains the following description of the rectory, gleaned from a number of different sources:

> The 'dining or common sitting-room', which 'looked to the front and was lighted by two casement windows', was perhaps to the right of the front door – the position of the chimney suggests a kitchen [as being] on that side of the house. The front door 'opened into a small parlour', where visitors were likely to find Mrs Austen 'busily engaged with her needle'. The larger room to the left may have been the Rector's study, looking to the garden, 'his own exclusive property ... But the study had a bay-window at the back of the house, and may have been wholly in the added part'.[6]

Where the Revd Austen's library was situated is not clear, but it is likely that the pupils' classroom (with dormitories above) was contained in one of the new extensions.

Servants at the rectory included a cook, a groom/coachman (the Austens kept a carriage and pair of horses), a nanny for the children, a housekeeper/lady's maid and a washerwoman.

In addition to the rectory, the property included:

> ... one barn ..., one lesser barn ... one close [enclosure] of gleib-land [glebe land] adjoining to the said parsonage house and barns, which is by estimation two acres & a half ... One parcel of gleib-land lying in the middle-common-field ... [which] is by estimation half an acre.

This area of 3 acres (which corresponds to plots 1, 2 and 3 as shown on the Plan of the Glebe Land of Steventon), served as part of the Revd George Austen's benefice. Also, the rector was entitled to tythes 'of what nature and quality soever, arising within the said parish', and to 'five eggs, payable on Good fryday' from every house within the said parish. For officiating at a marriage ceremony the rector's fee was 1s 6d, and for 'Churching of a woman' (taking a woman who has recently given birth to church for a service of thanksgiving), 6d. By 1727, however, the land adjoining 'ye Parsonage house' was recorded as being 1½ acres.[7] In addition, the Revd Austen farmed the 200-acre Cheesedown Farm, situated in the north of the parish.

At Steventon, George Austen occupied himself in his spare time by revising the Parish Register. (In this his daughter Jane would subsequently take a hand, albeit an unauthorised one, in making her own additions to the register, as will shortly be seen).

As a clergyman, George's income was a modest £100 per annum approximately, which was augmented by the profits from Cheesedown Farm. This income was further increased when he took in pupils from well-to-do families – half a dozen or so in number who boarded at the rectory and whom he tutored, along with his own sons, prior to them being admitted to Oxford University. They included George (born 1757), son of Warren Hastings of the East India Company and subsequently Governor-General of Bengal, and Richard, son of William Buller, Bishop of Exeter.

When the Revd Hillman died in 1773, George became Rector of Deane as well as of Steventon; this living having been purchased for him by his Uncle Francis Austen of Sevenoaks, Kent, who, as already mentioned, had also paid for his education. Reverend Austen now received an extra £100 per annum in consequence.

Mrs Austen, in addition to her wifely duties, kept a 'Little Alderney' – a small fawn-coloured cow, the strain of which originated from the Channel Island of Alderney and which yielded rich milk and creamy yellow butter. She also had a 'nice dairy fitted up with a bull and six cows'.

According to author Maggie Lane:

At Steventon, the Austens . . . enjoyed one of those old-fash-ioned gardens in which flowers and vegetables jostled for space. The family were always experimenting with growing things: their strawberry beds were famous, and they were the first people in the neighbourhood to grow potatoes – to the aston-ishment of their parishioners, who had never seen or tasted that vegetable, and who could not be convinced that it was worth cultivating! Alongside this more homely branch of gardening, the Austens kept up with the fashionable improvements of their time: designing the carriage sweep, and planting trees to screen a farmyard, or to create sheltered walkways.[8]

With eggs from poultry kept in the yard, the Austens were largely self-sufficient in food.

In addition to socialising with those neighbours of theirs who were on the same social plane, the Austen family made, and received, visits to and from their relations in Kent, Bath and elsewhere. What with the Austen family, its servants, and the Revd Austen's pupils and visitors, the rectory was indeed a busy and bustling place. It became more so when Mrs Austen's eldest sister Jane, widow of Dr Cooper, Vicar of Sonning near Reading in Berkshire, died in 1783, whereupon her children Edward and Jane spent much of their time at Steventon.

The Austens came into contact with the nobility and gentry at balls, held by the owners of stately homes and set in large estates which comprised woodland, expansive lakes and extensive parkland complete with trees and grazing sheep and cattle. Such people included Lord Dorchester (Kempshott Park); the Earl of Portsmouth (Hurstbourne Priors); Lord Bolton (Hackwood Park); the Holders (Ashe Park); the Bigg Withers (Manydown Park); the Chutes (The Vyne, Sherborne St John); the Portals (Freefolk); the Harwoods (Deane House); the Bramstons (Oakley Hall, Overton), and others.

Besides these balls, it appears that the Austens established 'no great intimacy with any of the neighbours [with whom they] were upon friendly but rather distant terms'. Nonetheless, Jane herself, and probably the rest of the family, had 'a regard' for their neighbours and 'felt a kindly interest in their proceedings'.[9]

Beyond this largely tranquil and self-contained world was a wider one. In 1778, for example, 1,000 French prisoners of war were imprisoned at Winchester (France's King Louis XVI having declared war on Great Britain on 10 July). The following year, some 8,000 men were imprisoned at Andover and Basingstoke.

Dr John Lyford of Basingstoke sometimes visited Steventon in order to attend Mrs Austen who suffered from indifferent health; after which he joined the family for dinner and 'partook of our elegant entertainment'.[10]

In November 1800 there was great excitement in the Steventon household when some new furniture arrived. Jane said:

The tables are come & give general contentment. I had not expected that they would so perfectly suit the fancy of us all three [presumably herself, her mother and her father] or that we should so well agree in the disposition of them ... The two ends put together form our constant Table for everything, & the centrepiece stands exceedingly well under the glass [mirror];

holds a great deal most commodiously, without looking awk-wardly. The Pembroke has got its destination by the sideboard, & my mother has great delight in keeping her Money & papers locked up. The little Table, which used to stand there, has most conveniently taken itself off into the bed-room & now we are in want only of the chiffonier, which is neither finished nor come.[11]

This implies that the furniture had been hand-made to order.

֍ 3 ֍

The Young Jane Austen

Jane was born on 16 December 1775 at Steventon Rectory, which would be her home for the next twenty-four years. Her father, the Revd George Austen, expressed his delight at the new arrival and he wrote to his sister Philadelphia to say: 'We now have another girl, a present plaything for her sister Cassy [Cassandra], and a future companion'.[1] Undoubtedly Jane's mother, Mrs Cassandra Austen, was equally delighted.

According to Jane's nephew, James E. Austen-Leigh, Mrs Austen

> followed a custom, not unusual in those days . . . of putting out her babies to be nursed in a cottage in the village. The infant was daily visited by one or both of its parents, and frequently brought to them at the parsonage, but the cottage was its home, and must have remained so till it was old enough to run about and talk.[2]

Of her daughter Cassandra, Mrs Austen said:

> I suckled my little girl thro' the first quarter; she has been weaned and settled at a good woman's at Deane just eight weeks; she is very healthy and lively, and puts on her short pet-ticoats today.[3]

In the case of Jane (and probably Cassandra also), Deirdre Le Faye believes that the foster parents referred to were John and Elizabeth Littleworth of nearby Deane.

Anna Lefroy recalled that in a room on the first floor of the rectory, the youthful Jane and her sister made a dressing room [used for dressing and for the storage of clothes] 'as they were pleased to call it'. This 'communicated with one of a smaller size' where Jane and Cassandra slept:

I remember the common-looking carpet with its chocolate ground that covered the floor and some portions of the furniture. A painted press [wardrobe], with shelves above for books, that stood with its back to the wall next [to] the Bedroom, & opposite the fireplace; my Aunt Jane's Pianoforte – & above all, on a table between the windows, above which hung a looking-glass, 2 Tonbridge-ware workboxes of oval shape [made at Tunbridge Wells and at Tonbridge in Kent], fitted up with ivory barrels containing reels for silk, yard measures, etc. . . . But the charm of the room with its scanty furniture and cheaply painted walls must have been, for those old enough to understand it, the flow of native homebred wit, with all the fun & nonsense of a large and clever family.[4]

Jane learnt her letters and words using ivory tablets, on which was written a letter of the alphabet. A sampler – worked in various stitches as an indication of proficiency and intended to be framed and hung on the wall – embroidered by Jane, measured 10in by 11.5in. It portrayed a compilation of various phrases from *The Book of Common Prayer*, with her name and the date:

Praise the Lord oh my Soul and all that is within me
Praise his Holy Name as long as I live will I praise
The Lord I will give thanks unto God while I have
My Being sing unto the Lord oh ye Kingdoms of the
Earth sing praise unto the Lord Give the Lord the
Honour due unto his name worship the Lord with holy

Worship in the Time of trouble I will call upon the
Lord and he will hear me Turn thy Face from my
Sins and put out all my Misdeeds.

Jane Austen, 1797

Beneath the text are several trees, one of which has a bird sitting atop it, and the whole is surrounded by a patterned motif.[5] She also made herself clothes and hats, including a cap decorated with lace for indoor use which was worn with ribbons, the colours of which were chosen according to the occasion.

Jane was visited at the rectory by her music master George William Chard, assistant organist at Winchester Cathedral, who rode the 14 miles from that city to Steventon in order to teach her and, presumably, other pupils in the area. Jane said, 'I practice [*sic*] every day as much as I can – I wish it were more for his sake'.[6] She practised the pianoforte each morning before breakfast, and entertained visitors with her playing whenever the occasion demanded it. She also spent time collecting songs and musical scores which she copied into her music book. She enjoyed singing, and a favourite song of hers which she loved to sing was by Scottish poet and songwriter Robert Burns entitled *Their Groves O' Sweet Myrtle*:

Their groves o' sweet myrtle let foreign lands reckon
Where bright-beaming summers exalt the perfume
Far dearer to me yon glen o' green breckan
Wi' the burn stealing under the lang yellow broom.

When Cassandra was sent at the age of 8 to a small, private school in Oxford, Jane, despite her tender age, insisted on joining her there. The school subsequently moved to Southampton where Jane and Cassandra were both taken ill with sore throats (possibly caused by diphtheria), whereupon their mother took them back to Steventon to be nursed back to health. They were then sent to a boarding school in Reading where Jane remained until she was 11. After this they were taught at home, availing themselves of their father George's his extensive library – with his permission.

Jane was taught French by Mrs Sarah Latournelle (*nèe* Hackitt), an Englishwoman who despite being married to a Frenchman could herself speak not a word of that language![7] Mrs Latournelle ran a school in the Forbury, formerly the outer courtyard of Reading Abbey.

George Austen encouraged his children, Jane included, to appreciate poetry and literature. For example, in the evenings it was his habit to read to them works by the English poet William Cowper (whom Jane, when she became a novelist, often quoted in her novels). As James E. Austen-Leigh said of the Revd Austen:

> Being not only a profound scholar, but possessing a most exquisite taste in every species of literature, it is not wonderful [surprising] that his daughter Jane should, at a very early age, have become sensible to the charms of style and enthusiastic in the cultivation of her own language.[8]

And William Austen-Leigh, in his book *Jane Austen: Her Life and Letters*, declared:

> Jane Austen inherited from her father her serenity of mind, the refinement of her intellect, and her delicate appreciation of style.[9]

Jane's brother Henry also encouraged her in reading and, according to him, her 'favourite moral writers were Samuel

Johnson in prose, and William Cowper in verse'.[10] This was not to say that Jane did not read the occasional raunchy novel, such as Henry Fielding's *The History of Tom Jones, A Foundling*, or even works showing the darker side of life such as Mathew Lewis's Gothic novel *The Monk*, featuring rape, incest and poisoning.

Jane's talent for writing manifested itself in the plays which she wrote as a child and dedicated to various members of her family, including her father George and her brother Edward, and also to friends. But being a playwright was not enough. She also took part, with her siblings, in amateur theatricals which were normally performed in the large barn, except at Christmas time when they were held in the rectory dining room. A play was chosen – for instance, *The Sultan* by Anglo-Irish playwright Isaac Bickerstaffe (whose real name was Jonathan Swift), which was enacted at Steventon in 1790 – for which eldest brother James would normally compose a prologue and an epilogue. Other plays which were performed included Mrs Susannah Centlivre's farcical comedy *The Wonder: A Woman Keeps a Secret*; Henry Fielding's *Tom Thumb* (a burlesque of the popular playwrights of the day), and the Revd James Townley's farce *High Life Below Stairs*.

Jane and her siblings helped their mother at the glebe farm where Mrs Austen's cattle were looked after by John Bond (born *c.*1738), the Revd Austen's bailiff. 'John Bond begins to find himself grow[ing] old', Jane told her sister Cassandra, adding playfully that this was something 'which John Bond ought not to do'. So it was thereafter decided that John was to confine himself to the less arduous duty of looking after the sheep.

Jane and Cassandra were in the habit of visiting and assisting those of their father's parishioners who happened to be poor and needy. One Christmas time, for example, Jane purchased for them items such as a shift (dress), a shawl and some pairs of worsted stockings with money provided by Steventon's squire, Edward Knight of Godmersham Park, Kent.

Life was not all work and no play – which is not to suggest that Jane regarded her writing as anything other than a pleasure. Favourite games which she enjoyed were cup-and-ball, at which Jane was reputedly an expert; the New Game of Emulation, played with dice where the object was to reach the final square on which an angel was depicted, and spillikins, where turns were taken with an ivory stick with a hook on its end to pick up other sticks from a pile, without disturbing them. Charades were also popular and were intended 'to enliven the long evenings . . . by merry verses and happy, careless inventions of the moment, such as flowed without difficulty from the lively minds of those amongst whom she lived'.[11]

Not only Jane, but also her mother and father, and brothers James, Henry, and Francis, invented brain-teasing conundrums. The following is a somewhat macabre one, composed by Jane, where the reader is invited to guess to what the author is referring:

When my first is a task to a young girl of spirit
And my second confines her to finish the piece,
How hard is her fate! But how great is her merit
If by taking the whole she effect her release!

And the answer to the conundrum is 'Hemlock'!

Jane and Cassandra enjoyed walking to Deane to visit their friends Mary and Martha Lloyd – a journey which Jane particularly relished when the 'hard, black frosts lay on the ground'.[12] Anna Lefroy remembered how, on the walks through the lanes, Jane and Cassandra wore 'pattens' (shoes with raised soles intended to protect the dress when the wearer walked outdoors on muddy ground), which were 'usually worn at that time, even by Gentlewomen. I remember too their bonnets [which were] precisely alike in colour, shape & material'.[13]

Jane also enjoyed visiting nearby Overton where she made purchases from a 'Scotchman' (a person, not necessarily Scottish by nationality, who was a doorstep seller of fabric and drapery goods):

> The Overton Scotchman has been kind enough to rid me of some of my money, in exchange for six shifts and four pairs of stockings. The Irish [linen] is not so fine as I should like; but as I gave as much money for it as I intended, I have no reason to complain. It cost me 3s 6d per yard.[14]

Balls were held in the Town Hall at Basingstoke, where the Master of Ceremonies introduced the guests and initiated the proceedings by leading one of the young ladies out onto the floor. Minuets, quadrilles and 'Roger de Coverley' were favourite dances of the day. The most favourite dance, however, was the polka, and this was undoubtedly on account of its having been forbidden at Court – ladies not being expected to reveal as much of their legs as the dance required. Jane responded to this injunction by transcribing as many polkas as she could lay her hands on into her music book, and playing them on the pianoforte at every conceivable opportunity!

Jane had the good fortune to have a friend, Mrs Anne Lefroy (whose son Benjamin would marry Jane's niece Anna Austen), who was generous by nature and arranged many social gatherings at her home, which was not far from Steventon. Jane always felt at a certain disadvantage; she and her sister being obliged each to survive on a mere £20 a year allowance, given to them by their father for their personal expenses. This was until she earned money of her own through the sales of her books.

What did Jane actually look like? It was Anna Lefroy who gave this fine description of her:

Her complexion [was] of that rather rare sort which seems the peculiar property of light brunettes. A mottled skin, not fair, but perfectly clear & healthy in hue; the fine naturally curling hair, neither light nor dark; the bright hazel eyes to match, & the rather small but well-shaped nose. One hardly understands how with all these advantages she could yet fail at being a decidedly handsome women.[15]

4

Jane's Siblings

Jane's eldest brother James Austen, born in 1765, was ten years her senior. Like all of the Austens' sons, he was educated at Steventon by his father. When he was old enough he followed in his father's footsteps by entering St John's College, Oxford, where he became a Fellow. James was said to be 'well-read in English literature, had a correct taste, and wrote regularly and happily, both in prose and verse'. It was also said that he had 'a large share in directing her [Jane's] reading and forming her taste'.[1]

Jane's brother George Austen, born in 1766, was nine years her senior. Sadly, from an early age he suffered from fits (presumably epileptic) from which he 'never recovered sufficiently to take his place in the family'.[2] George spent his time as a boarder in the village of Monk Sherborne, 3 miles to the north of Basingstoke, where he was looked after and visited regularly by his parents.

Edward Austen, born in 1767 and eight years Jane's senior, is described as 'an excellent man of business, kind-hearted and affectionate; and he possessed also a spirit of fun and liveliness'.[3] Thomas Knight II (the son of the Revd Austen's patron Thomas Knight I), Edward's distant cousin and his wife Catherine, took a great interest in the young Edward and invited him to spend much time with them at their home, Godmersham Park in Kent. Subsequently, in 1783 Edward was legally adopted by the Knights (who were childless), on condition that he adopted their surname. Edward, in turn, would stand to inherit the Knights' estates of Godmersham, Steventon and Chawton.

Henry Thomas Austen, born in 1771, was also educated at St John's College, Oxford, where he too became a Fellow. Henry was described by Jane herself as being 'most affectionate & kind, as well as entertaining'. In return, Henry was unstinting in his praise and admiration for Jane.[4] He also encouraged her in her reading, as already mentioned.

Cassandra Austen, born in 1773 and therefore almost two years older than Jane, was Jane's only sister. Jane's love and affection for Cassandra is evident from the dozens of letters which she wrote to her during her lifetime, signing herself 'With best love'; 'God Bless you'; 'Yours affectionately'; 'Yours ever'. In these letters she speaks of outings she has had, gives detailed descriptions of purchases which she has made of fabric – out of which clothes were to be made for forthcoming balls – and offers delightful snippets of family news such as, '. . . my father wishes to receive some of Edward's pigs'.[5] This appears to have been a two-way process because Jane subsequently tells Cassandra that the Revd Austen has furnished Edward with 'a pig from Cheesedown [Farm]; it is already killed and cut up, but it is not to [i.e. does not] weigh more than 9 stone; the season is too far advanced to get him a larger one'.[6]

When the sisters were apart they corresponded every three or four days. However, it was invariably Jane who made the first move. If Jane was the traveller, for instance, 'There [was] always a first letter from Jane telling Cassandra of the journey'. On the other hand, if Cassandra was the traveller, 'then the first letter is from Jane expressing the hope that she had a good journey'.[7] This suggests that of the two, Cassandra was emotionally the stronger and Jane the more dependent.

Francis William Austen ('Frank'), born in 1774, was a mere twenty months older than Jane. William Austen-Leigh said of him: 'There can be no doubt that by his bright and lovable nature he contributed greatly to the happiness of his sister Jane'.[8] At the age of 12, Francis joined the Royal Navy.

Charles John Austen, born in 1779, was three years younger than Jane. Jane referred to him as 'our own, particular little brother' – on account of him being the youngest. William Austen-Leigh remarked upon Charles's 'sweet temper and affectionate disposition, in which he resembled his sister Jane'. Said he:

> Charles Austen was one of those happy mortals destined to be loved from childhood to old age by every one with whom they [he] came into contact.[9]

At the age of 12, Charles too joined the Royal Navy.

Steventon lay in the territory over which the Vine Hunt operated, William John Chute of The Vyne, Sherborne St John, being Master of Foxhounds. Not surprisingly, therefore, hunting loomed large in the lives of Jane's brothers. In fact, it was said of George Austen that:

> all his own boys hunted at an early age on anything they could get hold of, and Jane, when five or six, must often have gazed with admiring, if not envious, eyes at her next oldest brother, Frank, setting off for the hunting field at the ripe age of seven, on his bright chestnut pony Squirrel (bought by himself for £1.12s).

For this he dressed in a suit of scarlet cloth made for him 'from a riding habit which had formed part of his mother's wedding outfit'.[10]

✿ 5 ✿

Enter Eliza Hancock

It was in 1786 that Eliza Hancock, Jane's cousin who was fourteen years her senior, appeared at Steventon Rectory like a brilliant comet, to bring life, gaiety and a certain degree of raciness to the proceedings. Eliza was the daughter of Philadelphia, George Austen's sister and her husband Tysoe Saul Hancock. Her life was, and would become, so extraordinary as to make Mrs Radcliffe's gothic novels – which Jane so despised – pale into insignificance. This was not least because Eliza's life was real and tangible.

Eliza's arrival occurred just as Jane was about to embark upon her teenage writing years, when she would produce her so-called *Juvenilia*, and her influence on this, and upon other aspects of her young cousin Jane's formative years, has probably been underestimated. In the words of James E. Austen-Leigh, Eliza was 'one of Jane Austen's most colourful connections and a significant influence on her teenage years'.[1]

Eliza's recent family history was as follows. Her mother Philadelphia, having been brought up, allegedly, in Hertfordshire by her maternal cousins, spent five years as an apprentice to a London milliner before sailing, in January 1752, to Madras. William Austen-Leigh declared:

That Philadelphia Austen went to seek her fortune in India is certain, and that she did so reluctantly is extremely likely. She had at an early age been left an orphan without means or prospects and the friends who brought her up may have settled the matter for her.[2]

In February the following year, Philadelphia met Tysoe Saul Hancock, son of a vicar from Hollingbourne in Kent. Hancock, who had worked in India since 1745, was an employee of the Honourable East India Company (HEIC). He and Philadelphia were married on 22 February 1753.

In 1759 Hancock was appointed as the HEIC's official surgeon at Fort St David, the company's military post near Madras. Here he met and became friends with Warren Hastings, also an employee of the HEIC (and subsequently, from 1773–85, Governor-General of Bengal). Hastings' wife – whom he had married two years previously in 1757 – was Mary Buchanan, who happened to be a friend of Philadelphia. By Mary, Hastings had one surviving son, George, born in December that year. Sadly, however, Mary died in July 1759.

In 1761 Hastings sent his son George – a sickly child now aged 3 – to England from India, to the Leigh family home at Adlestrop, Gloucestershire. Then, when Philadelphia's brother the Revd Austen married Cassandra Leigh in 1764, the couple brought George to live with them at their new home at Deane. George then became Revd Austen's pupil and he also 'came under Mrs Austen's maternal care'.[3]

On 22 December 1761 in Calcutta, the Hancocks' daughter Elizabeth – initially known as 'Betsy' and later as 'Eliza' – was born. She was their only child and Warren Hastings was invited to become her godfather.

In autumn 1764 Warren Hastings was struck by another tragedy when his son George died. According to William Austen-Leigh, Mrs Austen mourned George Hastings' death 'as if he had been a child of her own'.[4]

In 1765 Hancock returned to England with his wife and daughter. In 1769 he returned to India, leaving Philadelphia and Eliza in England, where they spent a great deal of their time with the Austens at Steventon. Hancock now engaged himself in business ventures, but when he failed to prosper, Warren Hastings came to the rescue by donating the sum of £5,000 (which he later increased to £10,000), 'in trust for Hancock and his wife during their lives, and, on the death of the survivor, to Betsy'.[5]

In the new year of 1773 Philadelphia visited Steventon to assist Mrs Austen, who gave birth to her fifth child Cassandra on 9 January 1773. Philadelphia's husband died in India in November 1775, whereupon Philadelphia went abroad. She and Eliza finally settled in Paris where the latter completed her education, paid for by the money which Hastings had given them (Eliza's father having died a bankrupt). Eliza's beauty, education and accomplishments, which included musicianship and the ability to speak fluent French and probably Italian, then became a passport for her entry into the upper echelons of Parisian society.

On 16 May 1780 Eliza wrote to her cousin, Philadelphia ('Phylly') Walter, from Paris, where she was clearly having a wonderful time:

> Paris is . . . the city in the world the best calculated to spend the whole Year in . . . We were a few days ago at Versailles & had the honour of seeing their Majesties & all the royal family dine & sup. The Queen is a very fine Woman, She has a most beautiful complexion & is indeed exceedingly handsome . . .

Eliza goes on to describe the queen's apparel:

> [her] Petticoat of pale green Lutestring [a glossy silk fabric], covered with a transparent silver gauze, [its] sleeves puckered

& confined in different places with large bunches of roses, an amazing large bouquet of White lilac . . . Feathers, ribbon & diamonds intermixed with her hair . . . Her neck was entirely uncovered & ornamented by a most beautiful chain of diamonds . . . The King was plainly dressed, he had however likewise some fine diamonds.

Eliza was, nevertheless, rather scathing about the Parisiens' wigs:

Powder is universally worn, & in very large quantities, no one would dare to appear in public without it, the Heads in general look as if they have been dipped in a meal tub.[6]

The relationship between Eliza and the Revd Austen was a close one and she would later say of him: 'What an excellent & pleasing Man he is, I love him most sincerely as indeed I do all the Family'.[7] Eliza sent her uncle, who was also one of her trustees, a portrait of herself in miniature.[8] However, on learning that she intended to marry French aristocrat Jean-François Capot, Comte de Feuillide and an officer in the Queen's regiment of dragoons, the Revd Austen was not amused:

Mr Austen is much concerned at the connexion, which he says is giving up all their friends, their country, and he fears their religion.[9]

Despite this, in late 1781 Eliza, then aged 20, and the Comte were married.

On 27 March 1782 Eliza, now the Comtesse de Feuillide, wrote to Phylly to tell her more about Paris:

I have danced more this winter than in all the rest of my life put together. Indeed I am almost ashamed to say what a racketing life I have led . . . Paris has been remarkably gay this year on account of the birth of the Dauphin [the eldest son of King Louis XVI and Queen Marie Antoinette]. This event was celebrated by illuminations, fireworks, balls etc. The entertainment of the latter kind given at court was amazingly fine. The Court of France is at all times brilliant but on this occasion the magnificence was beyond conception.[10]

Sadly, the Dauphin lived for only one year. In that same year, at Phylly's request, Eliza presented her with a miniature portrait of herself and a sample of her dark brown hair. On the back of the portrait were inscribed the words, *Amoris et Amicitiae* ('Of Love and Friendship').[11]

On 1 May 1783, Eliza tells Phylly how she has been to Longchamps, a monastery situated in the Bois de Boulogne where:

Devotion has given place to Vanity. Every Body now goes to Longchamps not to say their Prayers but to shew their fine Cloaths & fine Equipages . . . The number & magnificence of the Carriages are incredible.[12]

On 25 June 1786, while she and her mother Philadelphia were at Calais, en route from France to England, Eliza gave birth, prematurely, to a son, Hastings François Louis Henrie Eugènie – his first name being chosen to honour Eliza's godfather, Warren Hastings. The three spent time in London where Eliza was accepted at Court, just as she had been in France. It was at Christmas time, 1786, that Eliza and her family travelled to Steventon and met Jane (then aged 11) and Cassandra for the first time.

At Steventon Eliza entertained the family with piano recitals, participated in the customary Austen family theatricals and gave an account of the French king, queen and court, and of the splendours of Versailles. She also described the daring achievements of Jean Pierre François Blanchard who, on 2 March 1784 – as she herself had witnessed – had soared high above the French capital in his hydrogen-filled balloon. He had 'ascended to the height of 1500 fathoms & returned from thence in perfect health & safety to the astonishment of most of the Spectators'.[13]

James E. Austen-Leigh describes Eliza as 'a clever woman and highly accomplished, after the French rather than the English mode', and who could speak the French language perfectly.[14] It appears that Eliza was determined that Jane should become equally fluent because on 16 December 1786, which was the occasion of Jane's 11th birthday, she and her mother presented the young cousin with a copy of French children's author Arnaud Berquin's *L'Ami des Enfants* (a book which was designed to help British children learn French).

The outcome was, in the words of Anna Lefroy, that both Cassandra and Jane came to read French 'easily' and that 'in these matters I think it probable they had very valuable assistance from their cousin . . . [Eliza] who was an extremely accomplished woman, not only for that day, but for any day'.[15] And it was James E. Austen-Leigh's opinion that Jane and Cassandra 'may have been more indebted to this cousin than to Mrs La Tournelle's [*sic*] teaching for the considerable knowledge of French which they possessed'.[16]

It was undoubtedly Eliza, also, who encouraged Jane to sing in French, one of Jane's favourite songs being 'a little French ditty', the first two lines of which were:

Que j'aime à voir les Hirondelles
volent ma fenêtre tous les jours

Jane was clearly much taken with Eliza, for in 1790 she dedicated one of a series of letters, included in her novel *Love and Freindship* (her spelling), to the countess. (Eliza may have told Jane about the miniature portrait of herself which she had previously given to Phylly, and Jane may have chosen this title for her novel from the words which were inscribed on the back of it – in French, as previously mentioned). The letter was entitled, 'Deceived in Freindship and Betrayed in Love', and the dedication read:

> To Madame la Comtesse
> DE FEVILLIDE
> this Novel is inscribed
> by her obliged Humble
> Servant The Author.

❦ 6 ❧

Jane's *Juvenilia*

A useful insight into the character of Jane Austen is gained from a study of the short pieces of fiction – known as her *Juvenilia* – which she wrote in her early years between 1787 when she was aged 12, and 1793 when she was aged 18. Some of these pieces are written in the form of novelettes. For example, *Jack & Alice: a Novel*, consists of nine chapters, and is fifteen pages (of modern type) in length. Despite the tenderness of her years, these works reveal her enormous talent as a writer in the making, with a sense of the ridiculous coupled with an ability to entertain and make her readers laugh with her ready wit. Also, her *Juvenilia* contains many of the themes which she would, one day, expand on in the great novels which made her famous, and the tension which is at the heart of such novels; that tension between, say, conventionality and spontaneity; licentiousness and morality; genuineness and humbug; true love and affectation.

In *Frederic & Elfrida* (also described by her as a 'novel', even though it was only seven pages in length), Jane shows early signs of elegance and style of writing while describing a walk taken

> in a Grove of Poplars which led from the Parsonage to a verdant Lawn enamelled with a variety of variegated flowers & watered by a purling Stream brought from the valley of Tempé by a passage underground.

Love and Freindship, written in 1790, is described by Jane as 'a novel in a series of Letters'. In it, she takes pleasure at poking fun at established conventions. In the first letter, Isabel congratulates Laura on attaining the 'safe' age of 55:

If a woman may ever be said to be in safety from the determined Perseverance of disagreeable Lovers and the cruel Persecutions of obstinate Fathers, surely it must be at such a time of life.

In the fourth letter, Laura writes to Marianne warning her of the dangers of life in big cities. Laura quotes Marianne's mother who would often say:

Beware my Laura. Beware of the insipid Vanities and idle Dissipations of the Metropolis of England. Beware of the unmeaning Luxuries of Bath and the stinking fish of Southampton.

However, Marianne, who sees her mother as being over-protective of her, has other ideas:

'Alas!' exclaimed I. 'How am I to avoid those evils I shall never be exposed to? What probability is there of my ever tasting the Dissipations of London, the Luxuries of Bath, or the stinking Fish of Southampton? I whom [who] am doomed to waste my Days of Youth and Beauty in an humble Cottage in the Vale of Uske.' Ah! little did I then think I was ordained so soon to quit that humble Cottage for the Deceitful Pleasures of the World.

In *The History of England from the Reign of Henry 4th to the Death of Charles 1st* (1791), by 'a partial, prejudiced, and ignorant Historian', Jane demonstrates not only her knowledge of English history, but also that she is able to write about it in an amusing way. (This work by Jane is, in fact, a parody of a serious work in four volumes entitled *History of England* by Oliver Goldsmith). It is also clear that as far as characters and conflicts are concerned, she knows exactly whose, or which side she is on:

> Henry 4th ascended the throne of England, much to his own satisfaction, in the year 1399, after having prevailed on his cousin and predecessor Richard 2nd, to resign it to him, and to retire for the rest of his life, to Pomfret Castle, where he happened to be murdered.

During the reign of Henry V, 'Lord Cobham was burnt alive, but I forget what for,' says Jane. As for Henry VI, Jane has little good to say about him on the grounds that he was a Lancastrian; whereas the Duke of York 'was of the right side'. She then admits to her 'Hatred to all those people whose parties or principles do not suit with mine'.

In Henry VIII, Jane declares 'Anna Bullen' (Anne Boleyn) to be an:

> amiable Woman [who] was entirely innocent of the Crimes with which she was accused, and of which her Beauty, her Elegance, and her Sprightliness were sufficient proofs, not to mention her solemn protestations of innocence, the weakness of the Charges against her, and the king's character.

Henry's action in 'abolishing Religious Houses and leaving them to the ruinous depredations of time', had been 'of infinite use to the landscape of England in general, which probably was a principal motive for him doing it'.

As for King James I, Jane is 'necessitated to say' that in his reign the Roman Catholics 'did not behave like Gentlemen to the Protestants'. As she herself is partial to the Roman Catholic religion, she regrets that for this, she is obliged to blame the King (who was a member of the Roman Catholic Church).

Jane concludes that her principal reason for undertaking *The History of England* was to prove the innocence of Mary, Queen of Scots, 'and to abuse [Queen] Elizabeth'.

In Jane's novel *Catharine*, we find her pretending – as 'Miss Austen' – to be the patron of the works *Cassandra* and *The History of England*, rather than the author of them. The author writes to Miss Austen in gratitude for her patronage, telling her that both these books, through her generous support, had 'obtained a place in every library in the Kingdom, and run through three score Editions'. She, therefore, takes the liberty

> of begging the same Exertions in favour of the following Novel, which I humbly flatter myself, possesses Merit, beyond any already published, or that will ever in future appear, except such as may proceed from the pen of Your Most Grateful Humble Servt.

The author encloses a copy of her new work *Catharine* for Miss Austen's kind perusal. Catherine is an orphan who was brought up by a maiden aunt in a way which is immediately ridiculed. This aunt,

> while she tenderly loved her [Catharine], watched over her conduct with so scrutinising severity as to make it very doubt-ful to many people, and to Catharine among the rest, whether she loved her or not.

The result was that Catharine was:

> deprived of a real pleasure through this jealous Caution . . . to the extent of being prevented from going to balls because

a certain officer was to be there, or [of being required] to dance with a partner of her aunt's choice, rather than one of her own. [However] her Spirits were naturally good and not easily depressed, and she possessed such a fund of vivacity and good humour as could only be damped by some serious vexation.

Reading between the lines, this is Jane telling her readers that despite all obstacles, Catherine's great strength of character, derived from her inner resourcefulness, will prevail.

When a Mr and Mrs Stanley arrive, Catharine is pleased because this will 'relieve the dullness of the constant tête-à-tête with her Aunt'. Accompanying the Stanleys is their daughter Miss Camilla Stanley, for whom the past twelve years have been dedicated 'to the acquirement of Accomplishments which were now to be displayed, and in a few Years, entirely neglected'. The author of the novel is scornful of Camilla, declaring that:

> . . . those Years which ought to have been in the attainment of useful knowledge and Mental Improvement, had been all bestowed in learning Drawing, Italian and Music, more especially the latter, and she now united to these Accomplishments, an Understanding unimproved by reading and a Mind totally devoid either of Taste or Judgement. Her temper was by Nature good, but unassisted by reflection, she had neither patience under Disappointment, nor could sacrifice her own inclinations to promote the happiness of others. All her Ideas were towards the Elegance of her appearance, the fashion of her dress, and the Admiration she wished them to excite. She professed a love of Books without Reading, was Lively without Wit, and generally good humoured without Merit.

In other words, Camilla had wasted all the opportunities for betterment which had been presented to her.

Later in the story, Catharine ('Kitty') is seen by her aunt in the company of a young man called Edward Stanley, who suddenly seizes hold of her hand, presses it 'passionately to his lips', and runs 'out of the arbour [Aunt's garden]'. At this, the aunt has an apoplectic fit. Was this to be her reward, she asks, 'for all the cares I have taken in your Education; for all my troubles & Anxieties; and Heaven knows how many there have been!' Why, had she not brought her niece up virtuously, purchased for her Blair's *Sermons*, and Coeleb's *In Search of a Wife*; given her the key to her own library? All her aunt can say is that if Catharine feels shame for what she has done, is really sorry for it, and lives a future life of 'penitence and reformation', then perhaps she may be forgiven. 'I plainly see,' says her aunt, 'that every thing is going to sixes & sevens and all order will soon be at an end throughout the Kingdom.'

Here is Jane ridiculing the excessively pious and inflexible attitude of the aunt who, with her puritanical attitude, has no sense of humour, no sense of fun, and is absolutely determined to stand in the way of Catharine's future happiness.

In *A Collection of Letters*, Jane begins the first letter by putting herself in the position of a mother writing to a friend. As the children's first 'entrée into Life', the mother proposes to take them to tea with a Mrs Cope and her daughter. This will be followed by a week of further social engagements, including a private concert. 'How they will bear so much dissipation I cannot imagine,' she says.

Prior to the arrival of the carriage which is to convey them to Mrs Cope, the mother declares to her daughters that the moment has now arrived,

> when I am to reap the rewards of all my Anxieties and Labours towards you during your Education. You are this evening to

enter a World in which you will meet many wonderfull [*sic*] things; yet let me warn you against suffering yourselves to be meanly swayed by the follies and vices of others ...

However, her expectations are such that she says:

I can have nothing to fear from you – and can chearfully conduct you to Mrs Cope's without a fear of you being seduced by her Example or contaminated by her Follies.

Such is the excitement that when they reach 'Warleigh' (the home of the Copes), 'poor Augusta could scarcely breathe, while Margaret was all Life and Rapture ...The long-expected Moment is now arrived (said she) and we shall soon be in the World.' Here, Jane is obviously poking fun at the importance which parents attached to the prospect of their daughters' 'coming out' (entering society), and equally, to the daughters' exaggerated response to it.

In the second letter, Jane informs her friend Sophia that her (Jane's) husband had just been killed while fighting for his country in America, soon after which their three children had fallen sick and died. This was followed by the death of her father. To this Sophia replies:

Oh! My dear Miss Jane [she called herself 'Miss' in order to keep her marriage a secret from her disapproving father], how infinitely I am obliged to you for so entertaining a story! You cannot think how it has diverted me! But have you quite done?

To which the answer is no; for Jane goes on to say that her late husband Henry's elder brother has also died. 'Did you ever hear a story more pathetic?' asks Sophia. 'I never did', replies

Jane, 'And it is for that reason it pleases me so much, for when one is unhappy nothing is so delightful to one's sensations as to hear of equal misery'. Here is Jane, showing an insight into a common facet of human nature – being consoled in one's misfortunes, by the misfortunes of others.

The fourth letter deals with the subjects of friendship and happiness. When its young lady-writer asks Miss Grenville – who has recently arrived in Essex – whether she finds that county equal to the one which she has just left (Suffolk), the reply is: 'Much superior, Ma'am, in point of Beauty'. To which the young lady retorts: 'But the face of any Country however beautiful . . . can be but a poor consolation for the loss of one's dearest Friends'. Miss Grenville then declares that, 'Perfect Felicity is not the property of Mortals, and no one has a right to expect uninterrupted Happiness'.

In the fifth letter Jane's wit bubbles up to the surface again when Musgrove, cousin of Lady Scudamore, has harsh words to say against the laws of England, which allow uncles and aunts to remain in possession of their estates when their nephews and nieces are anxious to inherit them. If you were in the House of Commons [as a Member of Parliament], says he, 'you might reform the Legislature and rectify all its abuses'.

In her *Juvenilia*, Jane challenges existing conventions as any young person might, and brings the full power of her wit and invective to bear on that of which she disapproves; her humour even extending to serious topics such as death and bereavement.

In 1787, when she was aged only 12, Jane did something which can only be described as precocious, by making the following entries of her own in the Steventon Parish Register of Marriages. First, fantasising about her own future marriage, she proclaims:

> The banns of marriage between Henry Frederic Howard Fitzwilliam of London and Jane Austen of Steventon.

Next, she records that two other marriages had taken place:

> Edmund Arthur William Mortimer of Liverpool and Jane Austen of Steventon were married in this Church.

> This marriage was solemnised between us, Jack Smith & Jane Smith late Austen, in the presence of Jack Smith, Jane Smith.[1]

It says a great deal about the forbearance and sense of humour of her father the Revd George Austen, that these entries were allowed to stand and were not expunged from the register.

In December 1789 the 14-year-old Francis Austen, having completed his naval studies at Portsmouth's Royal Naval College, sailed aboard the Royal Naval vessel HMS *Perseverance* for the East Indies. In 1791, when Francis became a midshipman, his 12-year-old brother Charles followed in his footsteps as a pupil at the Royal Naval College, Portsmouth. A glittering career awaited them: Francis became Admiral of the Fleet and Charles, Rear Admiral and Commander-in-Chief of the East India and China Station.

In that year, 1791, the Revd Austen's uncle, Francis, died, leaving his nephew George the sum of £500. In December, Edward married Elizabeth Bridges and settled in a small house belonging to his wife's family and situated at Rowling, about a mile from her family home of Goodnestone Park in Kent. (Edward was the first of Jane's brothers to marry.)

In March 1792 James became the second of Jane's brothers to marry when he wedded Anne Mathew, daughter of General Edward Mathew, a former Governor of Granada. George Austen then made James his curate at Deane. Late in 1792 the Revd Tom Fowle, a former pupil of Jane's father, became engaged to Jane's sister Cassandra.

France declared war on Great Britain and Holland on 1 February 1793. Henry had intended to become a clergyman but he now changed his plans; he postponed his ordination and instead, on 8 April, enlisted as a lieutenant in the Oxford Militia. In 1797 he became Captain and Adjutant.

Thomas Knight II died in 1794. That September the 15-year-old Charles Austen left Portsmouth and joined HMS *Daedalus* as a midshipman. On 16 December, Jane's 19th birthday, her father, recognising her talents as a writer, purchased a mahogany writing desk for her for the sum of 12s.

On 3 May 1795 James's wife Anne Mathew died. In the same month, Francis sailed as a newly commissioned officer aboard the ship *Glory*, conveying troops of the 3rd Regiment of Foot to the West Indies. Lord Craven, who was Colonel of the regiment, invited Tom Fowle – his kinsman and Cassandra's fiancé – to accompany him on the voyage as his private chaplain. In the event Tom died of yellow fever at Santo Domingo in February 1797 and was buried at sea. In his will, he left Cassandra the sum of £1,000.

Jane lived vicariously through her brothers; their adventures were her adventures, their joys her joys, their heartaches her heartaches. This was particularly true of her naval brothers Francis and Charles. Whether they were thousands of miles away in foreign ports or on the high seas, or just down the road in Portsmouth, it made no difference.

In September 1796 Jane told Cassandra that Francis had received his appointment 'on Board the Captn John Gore, commanded by the Triton. . . .' Note that here she had amusingly transposed the name of the ship – *Triton* – and the name of its captain – Gore. The *Triton* is described by Jane as 'a new [type] 32 Frigate, just launched at Deptford. – Frank is much pleased with the prospect of having Capt. Gore under his command.'[2] This is another joke by Jane, for Francis is as yet a mere lieutenant who will not be made a commander for another two years. Jane is concerned for Henry, and in the same month she writes:

Henry leaves us to-morrow for [Great] Yarmouth [Norfolk], as he wishes very much to consult his physician there, on whom he has great reliance. He is better than he was when he first came, though still by no means well.[3]

✿ 7 ✿

Further Adventures of Eliza: Her Influence on Jane

Eliza's letter to Phylly, dated 9 April 1787, indicates that she is continuing to enjoy the high life. In just one day, for example, she had spent the evening at the Duchess of Cumberland's (wife of King George III's younger brother) and progressed 'from thence to Almacks [Assembly Rooms where balls of the most exclusive kind were held] where I staid till five in the morning . . . & am yet alive to tell You of it.' She added:

> I have been for some Time past the greatest Rake imaginable & really wonder how such a meagre creature as I am can support so much fatigue . . .[1]

That November, Eliza writes to Phylly in anticipation of a seasonal visit to Steventon Rectory:

> You know we have long projected acting this Christmas in Hampshire & this scheme would go on a vast deal better would You lend your assistance . . . Indeed My Dear Cousin your Compliance will highly oblige me & your declining my proposal as cruelly mortify me . . . I assure You we shall have a most brilliant party & a great deal of amusement, The House full of Company & frequent balls . . .

Here, Eliza is referring to the amateur theatricals which the younger generation of Austens were accustomed to holding at Steventon, usually in the great barn. In the event, Phylly declines the invitation.[2]

The theatricals duly went ahead in the Revd Austen's barn which was fitted up, according to Phylly, 'quite like a theatre'. All the 'young folks' took their part, the plays chosen being *Which is the Man?* and *Bon Ton*. 'The Countess [Eliza] is Lady Bob Lardoon in the former and Miss Tittup in the latter'.[3]

In the play *Bon Ton*, or *High Life Above Stairs: A Farce* by English actor, theatre manager and playwright David Garrick, Miss Tittup says:

> We went out of England, a very awkward, regular, good English family; but half a year in France, and a winter passed in the warmer climate of Italy, have ripened our minds to every ease, dissipation, and pleasure.

Surely this is an indication that Eliza had a hand in the choosing of it. As regards *Which is the Man?*, Phylly appears to be confused because Lady Bob [Bab] Lardoon features in a different play by English soldier and dramatist John Burgoyne entitled *The Maid of the Oaks*, or *A Fête Champêtre*, which is described as 'a cheerful little comedy of country life'.

On 22 July 1788 it was Phylly's turn to meet her cousins Cassandra and Jane for the first time. This was on the occasion of the latter's visit to their great-uncle Francis Austen at his home in Kent. Cassandra, said Phylly, 'bore a most striking resemblance of me in features, complexion & manners'. However, her comments about Jane were not complimentary. Jane was, said Phylly:

> not at all pretty & very prim, unlike a girl of twelve ... the more I see of Cassandra the more I admire [her] – Jane is whimsical & affected.[4]

Eliza, Hastings and Philadelphia spent the winter of 1788–89 in Paris. However, in the spring of 1789, with the summoning of the Estates General (which became the National Assembly), the French Revolution began. They therefore returned to London.

On 7 January 1791 Eliza wrote to Phylly from Margate, where she had taken her son who was not in good health. Here, she speaks of 'the great Benefit Hastings has received & still reaps from Sea bathing':

> I had fixed on going to London by the end of this Month, but to shew You how much I am attached to my maternal duties, on being told by one of the faculty whose Skill I have much opinion of that one month's bathing at this time of the Year was more efficacious than six at any other & that consequently my little Boy would receive the utmost benefit from my pro-longing my stay here beyond the time proposed, like a most exemplary parent I resolved undergoing the fascinating delights of the great City for one month longer and consequently have determined on not visiting the Metropolis till ye 28th of Febry. Was this not heroic?[5]

These scintillatingly witty lines could easily have tripped off the pen of Jane herself, for both ladies were able to write about serious matters in a light-hearted, even flippant way. This begs the question, did Jane model herself on the older Eliza in this respect?

On 26 February 1792 Philadelphia died. On 21 September of that year, when Eliza was staying with the Austens, France abolished its monarchy. The following day was declared the first day of the first year of the new French Republic. This was to have grave implications for Eliza's husband, as will soon be seen.

On 16 July 1792 Eliza wrote to Phylly concerning a 'little Accident' which she had recently suffered:

> I was attacked with a very violent fever & such a pain in my Head that I never have felt in my Life which for three Days & Nights nearly distracted me, at the end of this period a most violent eruption made its appearance and my Physician declared I had got the Small Pox. This I assured him could not be the case for I had had it, in short My Dear Friend for I would not quite tire you out with my dismal Story, my Disorder at length proved to be the Chicken Pox but which I had so severely that those about me all gave the comfortable assurance that I must be marked & completely frightful for the rest of my Days. This prediction however has not been exactly verified, at least I am not much more frightful than I was before, for the only trace now left of my Malady is one single mark in my forehead which as you may suppose does not make any violent alteration in my appearance.[6]

Here, Eliza is gently mocking the medical profession and Jane herself would also make sport of that profession in her forthcoming novels. Again, Eliza's writing is very reminiscent of that of Jane. It is not, of course, suggested that Jane was privy to her cousin's letters to Phylly; only that Jane may have derived inspiration either from Eliza's correspondence to her family, or from the latter's sparkling wit and repartee.

On 26 October 1792 Eliza wrote to Phylly from Steventon and remarked on the change which she had observed in the Austen sisters:

Cassandra & Jane are both very much grown (The latter is now taller than myself) and greatly improved as well in Manners as in Person both of which are now much more formed than when You saw them. They are I think equally sensible, and both so to a degree seldom met with, but my Heart gives the preference to Jane, whose kind partiality to me, indeed requires a return of the same nature.[7]

Like Jane, Eliza loved a ball. Unfortunately, however, she had been forced to miss 'a Club Ball at Basingstoke [held by the Hants Club whose members were a group of gentlemen from that town] and a private one in the neighbourhood [having] been confined to my Bed with a feverish Attack'. Nevertheless, she hoped to attend another ball on 4 November.[8]

On 21 January 1793 the French king, Louis XVI, was sent to the guillotine. (A few months later, on 16 October, his queen, Marie Antoinette, suffered the same fate). The French Republic declared war on Britain and Holland on 1 February. Like all French aristocrats, the Comte de Feuillide was now in mortal danger. When he attempted to bribe an official whom he hoped would look favourably upon his friend the Marquise de Marboeuf – who was then on trial for conspiring against the Republic – the Comte himself was put on trial. The outcome was that de Feuillide was condemned to death and guillotined, together with the Marquise, on 22 February 1794.

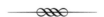

To return to Jane's *Juvenilia*, in it she did not neglect the subjects of love and marriage upon which, despite her inexperience in these matters, she wrote amusingly. First, she addresses the question as to what qualities a person might desire in a prospective partner. In *Jack and Alice* Mr Johnson suggests to Charles Adams, the owner of a large estate, that the latter might like to marry his daughter Alice. The response is in the negative:

> Your Daughter Sir, is neither sufficiently beautiful, sufficiently amiable, sufficiently witty, nor sufficiently rich for me – I expect nothing more in my wife than my wife will find in me – Perfection.

And what are the chances of meeting with such a partner? When Adams tells his cook Susan that his future wife, 'whoever she might be, must possess, Youth, Beauty, Birth, Wit, Merit, & Money', Susan declares that she has:

> many a time . . . endeavoured to reason him out of his res-olution & to convince him of the improbability of his ever meeting with such a lady . . .

But she confesses that her arguments 'have had no effect & he continues as firm in his determination as ever'.

Money and property loomed large when the choice of partner was being considered, and this theme was a favourite of Jane's in her later novels. When, in *The Three Sisters*, Mary asks Sophie, 'How should you like to marry Mr Watts?', the response is:

> Who is there but must rejoice to marry a man of three thou-sand a year (who keeps a postchaise & pair, with silver Harness, a boot before & a window to look out at behind)?

Jane, despite her youth, is aware of how easy it is, despite all preconditions, to fall in love with someone at first sight. In the fifth letter of *Love and Freindship*, Laura describes how she was suddenly and profoundly affected by the arrival of a stranger at her cottage. He was:

> the most beauteous and amiable Youth I had ever beheld. No sooner did I first behold him, than I felt that on him the happiness or Misery of my future Life must depend.

In the fifth letter of *A Collection of Letters*, a young lady receives a letter from Musgrove, cousin of Lady Scudamore, who declares:

> It is a month today since I first beheld my lovely Henrietta ... Never shall I forget the moment when her Beauties first broke on my sight – no time as you well know can erase it from my Memory.

To some people there are more important things to worry about than love and matrimony. In *Sir William Mountague*, for example, Jane describes how Sir William, at the age of about 17, inherits from his father Sir Henry, 'an ancient House & a Park well stocked with Deer'. Shortly afterwards he falls in love with three young ladies at the same time, and as he does not know which one he prefers, he leaves the county and retires to a small village 'in the hope of finding a shelter from the Pain of Love'. Here, he meets 'a young Widow of Quality' who consents to become his wife. However, when she names the date of the wedding as 1 September (the beginning of the game-bird shooting season), Sir William, being a fine shot, 'could not support the idea of losing such a Day, even for a good Cause'. The result is that the wedding is cancelled, but Sir William has the consolation of knowing, 'that he should have been much more grieved by the loss of the 1st of September ...'

Jane is not averse to poking fun at the matrimonial state. For example, in *Frederic & Elfrida*, Charlotte enters into a matrimonial engagement with two gentlemen at the same time; in *The Adventures of Mr Harley*, Harley, having been absent from England for half a year, finds himself in a stagecoach travelling to Hogsworth Green, 'the seat of Emma'. In the stagecoach with him are 'a man without a Hat, Another with two, An old maid & a young Wife [of] about 17 with fine dark Eyes & an elegant Shape'. It was then that Harley remembers that this latter person was 'his Emma [whom] he had married . . . a few weeks before he left England'.

Even in her twenties Jane continued to write amusingly about love and marriage – in fact, she was to do so all her life, both in her novels and in her letters. On 5 September 1796, for instance, she beseeches Cassandra to:

Give my Love to Mary Harrison [of Andover; a one-time lady friend of Jane's brother James], & tell her I wish whenever she is attached to a young Man, some respectable Dr Marchmont may keep them apart for five Volumes.

(Dr Marchmont is a fictitious character in Frances ('Fanny') Burney's novel *Camilla*, or *A Picture of Youth*, who interfered in the relationship between Camilla and her young gentleman friend).

On 15 and 16 of the same month, Jane writes to Cassandra skittishly:

Mr Children's two sons [of Tonbridge, Kent] are both going to be married, John & George. They are to have one wife between them; a Miss Holwell, who belongs to the Black Hole at Calcutta. [This, of course, is a pun by Jane on the word 'hole'.][9]

It is impossible for the independent observer not to find similarities, both of style and of content, in the works of Jane Austen and her cousin Eliza. In both are to be found scintillating wit, together with a readiness to ridicule antiquated traditions, conventions or views. And just as Eliza has the refreshing ability to make a joke at her own expense, so Jane does likewise, albeit vicariously through the characters of her novels. All this is set against a background of literary knowledge. (Eliza, like Jane, was well versed in poetry, quoting, for example, in her letters to Phylly, from Alexander Pope and Matthew Prior. She was also familiar with the plays of Shakespeare and the operas of Mozart).[10]

One may imagine Eliza at Steventon, sharing Jane's sense of humour and acting as a catalyst by giving Jane the confidence to write uninhibitedly about situations which she found to be interesting, amusing or absurd. Indeed, it may not be too much of an exaggeration to say that Jane modelled herself, to some extent in her writing, on Eliza.

It appears that Eliza not only had a profound effect on Jane, but also on her brothers James and Henry, both of whom are alleged to have fallen in love with her. But when Henry proposed to her in 1795, she refused him.

🌿 8 🌿

Romance: Tom Lefroy and Edward Bridges

In a letter to her sister Cassandra dated 9/10 January 1796, Jane, in her first sentence, mentions the fact that yesterday was Tom's birthday. The 'Tom' referred to was Thomas Langlois Lefroy and it was, in fact, his 20th birthday – Jane having celebrated her 20th birthday in the previous month of December (1795).

The Lefroy family, which was of Huguenot decent, had settled in Kent in the late sixteenth century. Tom's father, Antony Peter Lefroy, was an army officer. He was not a wealthy man and his commission had been purchased for him by his maternal uncles of the name Langlois. Anthony was stationed in Ireland where, in 1765, he married Anne Gardiner, daughter of a local squire. The couple had ten children; Tom being the eldest of five sons.

Jane Austen had first met Tom Lefroy in the autumn or winter of 1796 when he was staying with his uncle the Revd (Isaac Peter) George Lefroy and aunt Anne (*née* Bridges) at Ashe, a village 2 miles north of Steventon. The Revd George Lefroy was also indebted to his forebears for it was his uncle, the wealthy diplomat Benjamin Langlois, who had purchased for him his livings of Ashe and Compton, which he held in plurality.

The Lefroys had arrived in Hampshire from Surrey in 1783 (when Jane Austen was only 8 years old). Mrs Lefroy was a philanthropist with a great interest in public health and social work. She also loved to host social events, and she and Jane became great friends, despite a disparity in their ages of twenty-six years. When Jane first met him, Tom Lefroy had just completed his law studies at Trinity College, Dublin – his great-uncle Benjamin Langlois having provided the funds for his education. Tom was shortly to enter Lincoln's Inn, one of London's four Inns of Court to which barristers belonged and from which they were called to the Bar. Jane's introduction to Tom was an event which was to change her life, at first for better, and shortly afterwards, for worse.

In her above-mentioned letter to Cassandra, Jane goes on to describe 'an exceedingly good ball' which she had attended the previous evening, and declares that she is almost afraid to tell her sister:

how my Irish friend [Tom] and I behaved. Imagine to yourself everything most profligate and shocking in the way of dancing and sitting down together.

Jane declares that she can expose [i.e. make a spectacle of] herself in this fashion only once more because Tom is due to leave the country very shortly.

She assures Cassandra that Tom is a 'very gentlemanlike, good looking, pleasant young man'. She had encountered him at three previous balls, but apart from this, they had not met. Jane now makes a very telling comment that Tom:

. . . is so excessively laughed about [concerning] me at Ashe [Ashe Rectory – the home of the Lefroy family] that he is ashamed of coming to Steventon, and ran away when we called on Mrs [Anne] Lefroy a few days ago.

Why, it may be asked, did the household at Ashe laugh excessively about Jane, and why was Tom so ashamed of coming to Steventon?

Jane goes on to say that since the ball she has been visited by Tom and by his cousin George. George was aged 13 and Jane comments that he is 'really well-behaved now', implying that perhaps he had not been well-behaved on previous occasions! As for Tom, Jane declares that he has 'but one fault', which was that his morning coat was 'a great deal too light'. Jane believed that Tom had chosen a coat that was light in colour deliberately, because he was imitating Tom Jones (the novelist Henry Fielding's character in the book of that name) whom he greatly admired and who was wearing a white-coloured coat when he was wounded.

A few days later, on 14 January 1796, Jane writes again to Cassandra. The following evening there was to be a gathering at Ashe:

> I look forward with great impatience to it, as I rather expect to receive an offer from my friend in the course of the evening. I shall refuse him however, unless he promises to give away his white Coat.

The 'offer' clearly refers to an offer of marriage which Jane hopes to receive – undoubtedly from Tom Lefroy. For her, this is a most serious matter and yet, as is so often the case, she jokingly pretends that it is not.

Jane's letter to Cassandra is full of hope and expectation. She tells her sister that she is prepared to dispense with all her 'other admirers' and 'even the kiss which C. Powlett [the Reverend Charles Powlett] wanted to give me, as I mean to confine myself in future to Mr Tom Lefroy, for whom I do not care sixpence'.

This latter comment was, again, said tongue-in-cheek, for as will be seen, Jane cared for Tom a great deal. When she completes the letter the following day, however, she is in the depths

of despair; all her hopes having been dashed, for after that
gathering on Friday night at Ashe she would never see Tom
Lefroy again. She writes, sorrowfully:

> At length the Day is come on which I am to flirt my last with
> Tom Lefroy, & when you receive this it will be over – My tears
> flow as I write, at the melancholy idea.

Here, for once, Jane is unable to disguise her feelings by making
light of the situation. So why had Tom left under such unhappy
circumstances? The answer was given, many years later, by
Caroline Austen (daughter of Jane's eldest brother James, by
his second wife Mary Lloyd) in a letter that she wrote to her
brother James E. Austen-Leigh. (Caroline said that her remarks
were based upon what her mother had told her).

> Mrs [Anne] Lefroy sent the gentleman [Tom Lefroy] off at
> the end of a very few weeks, that no more mischief might be
> done. If his love had continued a few more years, he might
> have sought her [Jane] out again – as he was [by] then making
> enough to marry on – but who can wonder that he did not?[1]

On 17 November 1798 Jane told Cassandra of a conversation
she had had with Mrs Lefroy in which, 'of her nephew [Tom]
she said nothing at all ...'. In fact, Mrs Lefroy mentioned Tom's
name only once, but even when she did, Jane was 'too proud
to make any enquiries'. Afterwards, however, Jane learnt from
her father that Tom 'was gone back to London in [on] his
way to Ireland, where he is called to the Bar and means to
practise'.[2] (Tom had been called to the Irish Bar in the previous
year, 1797, after which he practised law in Dublin).

Caroline Austen declared that when Tom did finally marry
(in 1799) it was to 'an Irish lady – who certainly had the con-

venience of money . . .'. The lady referred to was Mary Paul, the sister of a friend of Tom's from college, who would bear him nine children. Caroline also stated that there had never been an engagement between Tom and Jane.[3] Helen Lefroy, in an article entitled *Strangers* which was published by the Jane Austen Society in 1982, begs to differ in respect of Mary Paul's financial situation. 'Mary,' she said, 'brought no great dowry to the marriage'. (Mary did, however, inherit the estate of Siversprings, County Wexford, on the unexpected death of her brother).[4] In 1852, Tom Lefroy became Lord Chief Justice of Ireland – a post which he held until his retirement at the age of 91.

Did Tom really intend to propose to Jane on that January evening in 1796, as she herself believed? If so, did Mrs Lefroy get wind of the fact, and was this why she packed him off to London in so summary a fashion? Whatever Mrs Lefroy and her husband, the Revd George Lefroy's thoughts and feelings on the matter may have been, they were well aware of the importance of acting in accordance with the wishes of Tom's family. Tom's parents, for example, surely hoped that their son would find a person of a higher social status than Jane – the daughter of a humble schoolmaster turned clergyman – to marry. And had not the wealthy Benjamin Langlois (Tom's great-uncle, to whom he was indebted for his education) purchased for Mrs Lefroy's husband his living at Ashe? Certainly, it would be most unwise to risk offending either of these two parties.

Perhaps Jane realised the predicament in which Mrs Lefroy found herself. In any event, she does not appear to have blamed Mrs Lefroy and the pair continued to be firm friends.

Nevertheless, it is surely no coincidence that in Jane's subsequent novels there can be found the theme of a rigid social class system, combined with interfering relatives or friends, being an impediment to the love and affection which two people feel for one another.

When, on 5 September 1796, Jane writes to Cassandra describing how she has dined at Goodnestone Park near Canterbury in Kent – the home of the Bridges family – there are indications that she has become attracted to another would-be suitor. At Goodnestone, Jane opened a ball with (Brook) Edward Bridges, the fourth son of the family.[5] (It will be remembered that in December 1791, Jane's brother Edward had married Edward Bridges' sister Elizabeth).

The next reference by Jane to Edward Bridges comes on 27 August 1805, when she writes to Cassandra from Goodnestone Farm to say that Edward (who is now Curate of Goodnestone) has arrived, unexpectedly, for dinner. She says:

> It is impossible to do justice to the hospitality of his attentions towards me; he made a point of ordering toasted cheese for supper entirely on my account. We had a very agreeable evening.[6]

When three years later, on 20 November 1808, Jane writes to Cassandra again, it is clear that the situation has completely changed. She says:

> Your news of Edw: Bridges was quite news, for I have had no letters from Wrotham [Kent, where Edward's sister Harriot,

[Harriet] who was married to its rector George Moore, lived]
– I wish him [Edward] happy with all my heart, & hope his
choice may turn out according to his own expectations, &
beyond those of his Family – And I dare say it will. Marriage is
a great Improver & in a similar situation Harriet [Foote] may
be as amiable as Eleanor [Harriet's sister]. – As to Money, that
will come You may be sure, because they cannot do without it.
– When you see him again, pray give him our Congratulations
& best wishes.[7]

Clearly, the 'news' to which Jane refers is the engagement
of Edward Bridges – now Rector of Bonnington, Kent – to
Harriet Foote. The following year, 1809, Edward and Harriet
were duly married.

On 26 October 1813 Jane, in a letter to Cassandra from
Godmersham Park, clearly believed that Edward had made a
bad match:

We have had another of Edward Bridges' Sunday visits. –
I think the pleasantest part of his married Life, must be the
Dinners & Breakfasts & Luncheons & Billiards that he gets in
this way at Gm [Godmersham Park]. Poor Wretch! He is quite
the Dregs of the Family as to luck.[8]

✤ 9 ✤

Pride and Prejudice

The novel began life as *First Impressions* (written by Jane between October 1796, when she was aged 21, and August 1797). It was revised in 1812, renamed *Pride and Prejudice* and published in January 1813 by Thomas Egerton.

Mr Bennet and his wife have five daughters and it is Elizabeth, the second of them, who is the principal character in the story. Of the other daughters, Jane, the eldest, makes the acquaintance of a Mr Bingley who rents a neighbouring country house and Lydia meets army officer Mr Wickham of the local militia. The book begins with the famous line, 'It is a truth universally acknowledged, that a single man in possession of a good fortune, must be in want of a wife'.

There is an abundance of humour in the story, beginning in the very first chapter with Mrs Bennet telling Mr Bennet that he has no compassion on her 'poor nerves'. To which he replies:

> You mistake me, my dear. I have a high respect for your nerves.
> They are my old friends. I have heard you mention them with
> consideration these twenty years at least.

At a ball, Mr Bingley introduces the assembled company to Mr Darcy who:

> ... soon drew the attention of the room by his fine, tall person,
> handsome features, noble mien; and the report which was in

> general circulation within five minutes after his entrance, of his having ten thousand [pounds] a year.

However:

> his manners gave a disgust which turned the tide of his popularity; for he was discovered to be proud, to be above his company, and above being pleased.

This is Jane Austen laying down the acceptable standards of good manners by which a prospective husband should be judged. Meanwhile, Lydia pursues the officers of the local militia with gusto. 'If we make haste, perhaps we may see something of Captain Carter before he goes'.

Mr Bennet's cousin and heir to the estate – which includes the abode of the Bennets (property in those days always descending through the male line) – is Mr Collins, a clergyman whose patroness is Lady Catherine de Bourgh, Darcy's aunt. Collins is described as having originally possessed 'great humility of manner', but this was now 'a good deal counteracted by the self-conceit of a weak head'. He declares admiringly that, 'he had never in his life witnessed such behaviour in a person of rank – such affability and condescension, as he had himself experienced from Lady Catherine'.

A favourite device of Jane Austen's is to place her hero – e.g. Darcy – in the position of being wrongly accused of some misdemeanour. This is so in *Pride and Prejudice*, where Wickham confides to Elizabeth Bennet that Darcy had failed to honour a promise he made; the promise being that he would provide for Wickham after his father's death. (Mr Darcy Senior being Wickham's godfather).

When Mr Collins makes a proposal of marriage to the unsuspecting Elizabeth, he gives his reasons for marrying as:

... first, that I think it a right thing for every clergyman in easy circumstances to set the example of matrimony in his parish. Secondly, that I am convinced it will add very greatly to my happiness; and thirdly ... that it is the particular advice and recommendation of the very noble lady whom I have the honour of calling patroness [i.e. Lady Catherine de Bourgh].

Needless to say, Elizabeth summarily declines his offer. Elizabeth's mother, who is extremely disappointed by her daughter's decision, now gives her an ultimatum in regard to her refusal of Mr Collins. Upon this ultimatum Elizabeth's father makes the following comment:

An unhappy alternative is before you, Elizabeth. From this day you must be a stranger to one of your parents. – Your mother will never see you again if you do not marry Mr Collins, and I will never see you again if you do.

Mr Collins speaks in glowing terms about Lady Catherine's home 'Rosings', and in sycophantic terms about the lady herself. When the Bennets are invited to 'Rosings' for a meal, he expresses the hope that 'so many servants, and so splendid a dinner might not wholly overpower them'. As for their attire:

I would advise you merely to put on whatever of your clothes is superior to the rest, there is no occasion for any thing more. Lady Catherine will not think the worse of you for being simply dressed. She likes to have the distinction of rank preserved.

When the Bennets are introduced to Lady Catherine they find her to be a highly opinionated woman. Elizabeth, however, is not to be put down. When her ladyship expresses astonishment that the younger Bennet sisters are 'out' [i.e. have entered society] before the elder ones are married, Elizabeth argues that this was not a sufficient reason for the younger ones to be denied 'their share of society and amusement'. When Lady Catherine tells Elizabeth that she will never play the pianoforte really well unless she practises more, even Darcy looks 'a little ashamed of his aunt's ill-breeding'. In other words, simply because Lady Catherine is who she is, this does not excuse her for being ill-mannered.

Elizabeth shows a similar determination not to be intimidated, this time by Darcy who approaches the pianoforte as she is playing and singing:

> You mean to frighten me, Mr Darcy, by coming in all this state to hear me? But I will not be alarmed . . . There is a stubbornness about me that never can bear to be frightened at the will of others. My courage always rises with every attempt to intimidate me.

Darcy falls in love with Elizabeth and tells her 'how ardently I admire and love you'. He also declares that, 'his sense of her [social] inferiority' causes him to be apprehensive and anxious. This, to Elizabeth, is like a red rag to a bull:

> I might as well enquire why with so elegant a design of offending and insulting me, you chose to tell me that you liked me against your will, against your reason, and even against your character?

Needless to say, Elizabeth refuses his proposal, just as previously she had refused the proposal of Mr Collins. However:

> the tumult of her mind was now painfully great. She knew not how to support herself, and from actual weakness sat down and cried for half an hour.

In discussing marriage, Elizabeth gives the relationship between her father and mother, Mr and Mrs Bennet, as an example of the pitfalls which may be encountered on entering that state of union:

> Her father, captivated by youth and beauty, and that appearance of good humour which youth and beauty generally give, had married a woman whose weak understanding and illiberal mind, had very early in their marriage put an end to all [of his] real affection for her. Respect, esteem, and confidence, had vanished forever, and all his views of domestic happiness were overthrown.

Meanwhile, Elizabeth's sister Jane, who has formed a romantic attachment to Bingley, learns that the latter has gone to London and will not be returning for some time. When Elizabeth discovers that Darcy has 'lately saved a friend' from a young lady against whom he [Darcy] had 'strong objections', she guesses that this is a reference to Bingley and her sister Jane, and she is greatly distressed.

When Darcy writes to Elizabeth explaining the truth about Wickham – that the latter had behaved extravagantly and dissolutely, and had attempted to elope with Darcy's sister Georgiana – she sees the error of her ways. Her behaviour, she says, has been 'blind, partial, prejudiced, absurd. How despicably have I acted! I, who have prided myself on my discernment!'

Elizabeth learns that her younger sister Lydia has eloped with Wickham and she feels guilty that she had been blind to the latter's true character. Not only that, but the event has wider implications:

> Her [Elizabeth's] power was sinking; every thing must sink under such a proof of family weakness, such an assurance of the deepest disgrace.

And because of this disgrace, she honestly feels that even though she could have loved Darcy, in these new and tragic circumstances 'all love must be in vain'. Mr Collins does not make matters easier when he writes to Mr Bennet about the elopement in a most unchristian way: 'The death of your daughter would have been a blessing in comparison of this.' When Lydia and Wickham are finally located, they consent to be married under the terms of an arrangement to be made with Mr Bennet, whereby the latter is to make a financial settlement on his daughter. It later transpires that Darcy had played a key role in persuading Wickham to marry, by purchasing for him a commission in the regular army, and also providing the sum of £1,000 for Lydia's dowry.

A subsequent meeting between Elizabeth and Wickham is cordial, in accordance with Jane Austen's philosophy that there is no such thing as a permanent enemy and life must go on, wherever possible, in peaceful co-existence. Elizabeth says, 'Come, Mr Wickham, we are brother and sister, you know. Do not let us quarrel about the past. In future, I hope we shall be always of one mind', whereupon he kisses her proffered hand 'with affectionate gallantry'.

A meeting with Lady Catherine provides Elizabeth with another opportunity of demonstrating her independence of spirit. When Elizabeth is asked to promise that she will never enter into an engagement with Darcy her response is: 'I will make no promise of the kind. I am not to be intimidated into anything so wholly unreasonable.' Her ladyship then tells her that she is an 'unfeeling and selfish girl'. To which Elizabeth retorts:

I am only resolved to act in that manner, which will, in my own opinion, constitute my happiness, without reference to *you*, or to any person so wholly unconnected with me.

When Darcy and Elizabeth take a walk together it is he who now expresses regret. The recollection of his conduct and manners, he says:

> ... has been many months, inexpressibly painful to me. Your reproof, so well applied, I shall never forget: 'Had you behaved in a more gentleman like manner.' Those were your words. You know not, you can scarcely conceive, how they have tortured me ...

Darcy also confesses to Elizabeth what she had already guessed: that he *had* interfered in the courtship of Bingley and her sister Jane; an interference which he now describes as 'absurd and impertinent'. Darcy had, at first, thought that Jane was indifferent to Bingley. However, he later changed his mind and now, being convinced of their affection he 'felt no doubt of their happiness together'. The story ends happily with the marriage of the two sisters: Elizabeth to Darcy, and Jane to Bingley.

In *Pride and Prejudice*, the heroine Elizabeth, highly conventional in many ways, is highly avant-garde in others. She sees no reason to suppose that Darcy is in any way her superior, simply because he is an aristocratic and landed person. Neither does she consider that his aunt, Lady Catherine de Bourgh, simply because of her status in society, has any right to make judgements about Elizabeth's younger sisters, or to interfere in her choice of a partner. In other words, a mere difference in social status should not take precedence over the love which two people feel for one another.

❦ 10 ❦

Sense and Sensibility

Sense and Sensibility, published in 1811 by Thomas Egerton, started life as *Elinor and Marianne*, written by Jane as a collection of letters in about 1795–96. However, the novel proper was begun in 1797 (and subsequently revised in 1811).

It is the story of two sisters, Elinor and Marianne Dashwood, and their differing reactions to love and rejection, for they are of very different natures. The book begins by describing the Dashwoods' home in Sussex and the family's position in society, which epitomises solidity, permanence and respectability.

> Their estate was large, and their residence was at Norland Park in the centre of their property where, for many generations, they had lived in so respectable a manner as to engage the general good opinion of their surrounding acquaintance.

Alas, this happy state of affairs was not to continue. Elinor, the elder of the two (in fact, there were three sisters altogether), is described as possessing 'a strength of understanding, and coolness of judgement', even though she was aged only 19. 'She had an excellent heart; – her disposition was affectionate, and her feelings were strong; but she knew how to govern them . . .' Marianne, on the other hand, whose 'abilities were, in many respects, quite equal to Elinor's', was:

sensible and clever; but eager in everything; her sorrows, her joys, could have no moderation. She was generous, amiable, interesting: she was everything but prudent.

When their father Mr Henry Dashwood dies, his estate passes to John – his son by his first wife. John and his wife Fanny move into Norland Park where Fanny's brother Edward Ferrars forms an attachment to Elinor. Elinor, for her part, declares that she thinks very highly of Edward and that she greatly esteems and likes him. Her sister Marianne, however, has reservations about him, saying that although he is very amiable, he 'has no real taste'. He was scarcely attracted by music and, although he admired Elinor's drawings, he failed to 'understand their worth'.

John fails to honour the promise which he made to his father; that he would look after his step-mother and sisters. Mrs Dashwood and her daughters, realising that they are now unwelcome in what had been their home, decide to relocate to Barton Cottage in Devonshire which is owned by their kinsman Sir John Middleton of Barton Park. When the time comes to leave, Marianne exclaims emotionally about Norland, 'When shall I cease to regret you! – when [shall I] learn to feel a home elsewhere!'

The sisters are introduced to Sir John's great friend Colonel Brandon whom Marianne regards as 'an absolute old bachelor, him being on the wrong side of five and thirty'. When the two sisters are out walking, Marianne sprains her ankle and falls to the ground, whereupon John Willoughby (described as a sportsman), who is out hunting with his gun, comes to the rescue. When Mrs Dashwood asks Sir John what kind of man Willoughby is he replies, 'as good a kind of fellow who ever lived, I assure you. A very decent shot, and there is no bolder rider in England'. (This is Jane humorously describing how two people can visualise a third from completely different perspectives!)

When Sir John suggests to Marianne that she will soon be setting her cap at Willoughby, Marianne scolds him saying:

> That is an expression, Sir John, which I particularly dislike. I abhor every common-place phrase by which wit is intended; and, 'setting one's cap at a man', or 'making a conquest', are the most odious of all.

Marianne, far from being overshadowed by her elder sister, is described as having 'never much toleration for any thing like impertinence, vulgarity, inferiority of parts, or even difference of taste from herself . . .'. Here she demonstrates that although the Dashwood family are dependent on Sir John's hospitality she, for one, does not intend to suffer the use of expressions which she considers to be both 'gross and illiberal'.

When Willoughby presents Marianne with a horse, Elinor expresses reservations about her sister receiving a gift from someone whom she has known for such a short time, and about whom she knows so little. To which Marianne replies haughtily:

> You are mistaken, Elinor, in supposing I know very little of Willoughby. I have not known him very long indeed, but I am better acquainted with him, than with any other creature in the world, except yourself and Mamma.

When Willoughby suddenly announces that he is departing on business to London, and has no idea when he will return, the effect on Marianne is devastating:

> [She] came hastily out of the parlour apparently in violent affliction, with her handkerchief at her eyes . . . This violent

oppression of spirits continued the whole evening. She was without any power, because she was without any desire of command over herself. The slightest mention of any thing relative to Willoughby overpowered her in an instant.

When Elinor, hitherto the more sagacious one, expresses the view that wealth has much to do with happiness, Marianne disagrees. It is her view that:

Money can only give happiness when there is nothing else to give it. Beyond a competence, it can afford no real satisfaction, as far as mere self is concerned.

When Edward Ferrars travels from Norland to visit the Dashwoods at Barton Cottage, and then disappoints them all by declaring that he is to go away, Elinor reacts in her typically controlled way. As soon as he is out of the house she sits down at her drawing-table and:

. . . busily employed herself the whole day, neither sought nor avoided the mention of his name, [and] appeared to interest herself almost as much as ever in the general concerns of the family.

Lucy Steele and her sister Anne, distant relations of Sir John, are invited to stay with him at Barton Park. Lucy drops a bombshell when she confides to Elinor that not only is she engaged to Edward Ferrars, but that she has been so for four years. At this news Elinor manages to maintain the composure of her voice, 'under which was concealed an emotion and distress beyond any thing she had ever felt before. She was mortified, shocked, confounded'.

Marianne is equally disappointed with Willoughby. When she writes to him, he responds by returning her letters and the lock of hair which she had given him and tells her that he is shortly to be married to Miss Grey, an heiress with £50,000. At this Marianne exclaims: 'Oh! How easy for those who have no sorrow of their own . . . Happy, happy Elinor, you cannot have an idea of what I suffer'. But when Marianne learns of Edward Ferrars' engagement to Lucy Steele she is filled with compassion for Elinor and says to her sister, 'What! – while attending me in all my misery, has this been on your heart? – and I have reproached you for being happy!'

Willoughby arrives on the scene to explain to Elinor the reason for his bad behaviour towards Marianne. 'I have been always a blockhead, I have not been always a rascal', he says. And then he declares that notwithstanding his affection for Marianne and despite her attachment to him, these factors were:

> all insufficient to outweigh that dread of poverty, or get the better of those false ideas of the necessity of riches, which I was naturally inclined to feel, and expensive society had increased.

In other words, for Willoughby, pecuniary considerations must take precedence over romantic feelings. Having heard how guilty and miserable Willoughby now feels about the whole business, Elinor's heart is softened – Jane Austen could never believe that any character (even one such as Willoughby) was wholly bad; everyone has *some* redeeming features.

Elinor's hopes of Edward Ferrars are dashed when she learns that he is married to Lucy Steele. However, when she and Edward meet, he explains that it is actually his brother Robert who has married Miss Steele. He then asks Elinor to marry him. All ends happily for Marianne also; she marries Colonel Brandon, and in doing so 'found that her own happiness in forming his, was equally the persuasion and delight of each observing friend'.

In *Sense and Sensibility* the sisters Elinor and Marianne react to setbacks in their romantic aspirations in different ways: the former calmly and stoically; the latter histrionically. And yet, both these coping mechanisms are effective in seeing them through to a happy ending.

The two sisters mirror the real life Jane and Cassandra Austen, who when they experience similar problems confide in one another and offer mutual support in precisely the same way. Also, Jane reflects the dread that insecurity can bring. She had doubtless heard how her father, the Revd Austen's great-grandfather John (born *c.*1670), had bequeathed his lands and estate entirely to his eldest grandson (also John), leaving his wife Elizabeth and their six sons and one daughter penniless. Jane would also have been aware of her father's own suffering when, as a child, he and his siblings were expelled from the family home by their step-mother Susanna Kelk.

On 17 January 1797 James was remarried to Mary Lloyd. In that year Thomas Knight II's widow Catherine, transferred to Jane's brother Edward, the Knights' adoptive son, Godmersham Park in Kent, and the estates of Steventon and Chawton in Hampshire, together with most of her late husband's fortune. This provided the latter with an income of £5,000 per annum. Meanwhile, Catherine retired to White Friars – a house in Canterbury.

July 1797 saw Eliza de Feullide debating with herself which of her 'variety of rural Plans . . . to adopt', one of her options being to 'retire into the embowering shades of the Rectory [i.e. Steventon]'.[1]

Jane and Cassandra visited Bath in November 1797 accompanied by their mother Mrs Cassandra Austen. Here, they stayed for about a month with Jane's aunt and uncle, James and Jane Leigh-Perrot (James being Mrs Austen's brother). The Leigh-Perrots were accustomed to spending about half the year in the city, where they rented a house at 1 Paragon Buildings. In the same month George Austen wrote to the London publisher Thomas Cadell, to inform them that he was in possession of a manuscript (Jane's novel *First Impressions*), and to see if they might be interested in publishing it. An answer in the negative was received.

Eliza finally accepts the hand of her cousin Henry Austen, and the couple are married on 31 December 1797. (Henry was the third of Jane's brothers to marry).

The Reverend Samuel Blackall

Jane Austen first met the Revd Samuel Blackall in the summer, or early autumn, of 1798 when he was staying with the Lefroys of Ashe. It is possible, in fact, that the meeting was arranged by Mrs Lefroy in an attempt to mitigate for Jane's disappointment over Tom Lefroy.

The Blackalls were a Devonshire family, the strangely named Offspring Blackall (1654–1716), Blackall's great-grand-father having been Bishop of Exeter in the time of Queen Anne. Blackall himself was a graduate of Emmanuel College, Cambridge, gaining his BA in 1791 and his MA in 1794, in which year he became a fellow of the college. In June 1794 he was ordained deacon at Ely in Cambridgeshire, and in December he was ordained priest. In 1796 he became Tutor and Proctor (officer with disciplinary functions) and in 1797, Taxor (imposer of taxes) at Emmanuel College. Shortly afterwards, he became College Steward and Librarian. At Emmanuel, Blackall was described as 'a sociable and lively member of the combina-tion room [fellow's common room]'. [1]

Jane wrote to Cassandra on 17 November 1798 telling her of a conversation she had had with Mrs Lefroy. A few weeks previously, said Jane, Mrs Lefroy had received a letter from:

> her [Mrs Lefroy's] friend . . . [the Revd Blackall, then aged 28] towards the end of which was a sentence to this effect: 'I am very sorry to hear of Mrs Austen's illness. [As previously men-

tioned, Jane's mother Cassandra did not enjoy good health.] It would give me particular pleasure to have the opportunity of improving my acquaintance with that family – with the hope of creating to myself a nearer interest. But at present I cannot indulge any expectation of it.'

Jane's reaction, on hearing this from Mrs Lefroy, was as follows:

This is rational enough; there is less love and more sense in it than sometimes appeared before, and I am very well satisfied. It will all go on exceedingly well, and decline away in a very reasonable manner. There seems no likelihood of his coming into Hampshire this Christmas, and it is therefore most probable that our indifference will soon be mutual, unless his regard, which appeared to spring from knowing nothing of me at first, is best supported by never seeing me.

Jane concludes by saying, 'Mrs Lefroy made no remarks on the letter, nor did she indeed say anything about him [Blackall] as relative to me'.[2]

From these remarks, it appears that Jane originally believed the Revd Blackall both cared about her and had regard for her. However, from his letter, she concluded that there was now 'less love' in their relationship, and that he was now indifferent to her. It is possible that in this she was mistaken, in that Blackall's not being able to 'indulge any expectation' of a further acquaintance may have been because a) he was many miles away in Cambridge, b) he had many duties to fulfil at his college, as has been demonstrated, and c) he was not in a strong enough position financially to support a wife. (Blackall's ambition, which he confided to Jane, was to acquire the 'exceedingly good' living of Great (North) Cadbury, in Somersetshire.[3] This, in those times, was worth 'a clear £800 per annum; he might have married on that ...').[4]

Jane has, therefore, convinced herself that the Revd Blackall is indifferent to her, but has she misinterpreted the meaning of Blackall's letter to Mrs Lefroy? After all, had he not openly affirmed his desire to improve his acquaintance with her family, in the hope of 'creating to myself a nearer interest'? And when Jane uses the words, 'very well satisfied' in regard to the outcome, may this not, in reality, disguise an inner irritation and disappointment?

To the outsider, Blackall – whose father, like himself, was a clergyman, and whose great-grandfather had been a bishop – as a man of learning and intelligence, would appear to have been the ideal partner for Jane. For her part she described him as 'a peice [*sic*] of Perfection, noisy Perfection himself which I always recollect with regard' – which, coming from one who did not bestow compliments lightly, was praise indeed! (The word 'noisy' may allude to the fact that Blackall was known to be a 'lively' and talkative character).

In early December 1798, Jane told Cassandra that their brother Francis had recently been at Cadiz where he was 'alive and well', he having written to her describing his adventures at sea.[5] On the 28th of that month, Jane became ecstatic. She told Cassandra:

> Frank [Francis] is made. – He was yesterday raised to the Rank of Commander, & appointed to the Petterel sloop, now at Gibraltar.[6]

Jane was as devoted to her younger brother Charles as to any of her brothers, though circumstances dictated that she saw precious little of him. James E. Austen-Leigh states that as an officer in the Royal Navy, Charles was absent from England [i.e. at sea] for a period of 'seven years together'.[7] Jane is constantly anticipating the next letter from Charles. She takes great interest in his fortunes, reporting, in late December 1798, that he 'is removed to the Tamer Frigate'.[8]

From August 1798 until March 1799, Cassandra enjoyed a prolonged stay at Godmersham Park with Edward and his family. At this time, Edward's health was giving cause for concern. Jane wrote:

Poor Edward! It is very hard that he who has everything else in the World that he can wish for, should not have good health too [and] I know no one more deserving of happiness without alloy than Edward is.[9]

Meanwhile, Jane developed a friendship with Martha Lloyd. Martha was the daughter of the late Revd Nowis (or Noyes) Lloyd who, prior to James becoming curate of Deane in 1792, had lived with her mother Martha (senior) at Deane parsonage. The Lloyds now lived at Ibthorpe, some 20 miles away. In a letter to Cassandra from Steventon, dated 18/19 December 1798 Jane, who perhaps wishing that she could be at Godmersham Park and enjoying the high life, declared irritably:

People get so horribly poor & economical in this part of the World, that I have no patience with them.– Kent is the only place for happiness, Everybody is rich there.[10]

On the surface, these remarks sound callous in the extreme, but they should be seen in the context of Jane's frustration at having to subsist on the small allowance paid to her by her father George. Also, it would not have escaped her notice that two of her brothers, James and Edward, had acquired wealth and property: the first through marriage, and the second through being adopted by a wealthy family.

✿ 12 ✿

Northanger Abbey

Northanger Abbey, written in 1797–98, began life as *Susan*. It was revised in 1802–03 and again in 1815–16 under the title *Catherine*. (The novel was finally published in 1818, after Jane's death, by John Murray). In *Northanger Abbey*, Jane makes the Gothic novel – a type of romance popular in the eighteenth and early nineteenth centuries – the target of her wit and satire. In the words of author J.M. Evans she:

> parodied those people who loved thrills and gorged themselves mentally with mysteries – strange noises, confessions of murders found in chests, secrets hidden in cabinets . . . etc.[1]

The heroine is 17-year-old Catherine Morland, the daughter of a clergyman. She is described as plain, awkward, inattentive and always preferring those enjoyments which she was forbidden to take. As for Catherine's mother:

> she had three sons before Catherine was born; and instead of dying in bringing the latter into the world, as any body might expect, she still lived on – lived to have six children more . . .

So here is Jane, on the very first page of the novel, treating the prospect of death in a humorous and witty way. (Death in childbirth, of course, was a common occurrence in her day).

When she was young, Catherine had no objection to books provided that 'nothing like useful knowledge could be gained from them [and] provided that they were all story and no reflection'. From the age of 15, however, her tastes become more refined as she acquaints herself with authors such as Pope, Gray, Thompson and Shakespeare.

The Allens are friends of Catherine's family; Mrs Allen being described as a person:

> whose vacancy of mind and incapacity for thinking was such, that as she never talked a great deal, so she could never be entirely silent. . . .

When they decide to visit Bath in Somersetshire, where Mr Allen proposes to have treatment for his gout, Catherine is invited to accompany them.

Before they leave for Bath, Mrs Allen cautions Catherine 'against the violence of such noblemen and baronets as delight in forcing young ladies away to some remote farm-house [the object of which is not explained, but may be guessed at]'. As for her own daughter Isabella, Mrs Allen begs her always to wrap herself up 'very warm about the throat, when you come from the [Assembly] Rooms at night . . .'.

Despite Mrs Allen's over-protective attitude Catherine, from the outset, is on the lookout for excitement, and it is a disappointment to her that on the journey to Bath, 'Neither robbers nor tempests befriended them, nor [did they experience] one lucky overturn [of the coach]', whereby Catherine (as the heroine of the story) might be introduced to a prospective hero.

An inordinate amount of time and trouble is taken by Mrs Allen to make sure that she and her young charge Catherine are fitted out with the appropriate clothes; the result being that when the latter accompanies Mrs Allen and her husband to a ball, they do not arrive at the ballroom until late in the evening. This first visit is a disappointment on account of the Allens being strangers in the area and having no acquaintances there. When they attend the Lower Rooms, however, (both the Upper and Lower Assembly Rooms being used for dances and concerts) the Master of Ceremonies introduces Catherine to a Mr Henry Tilney, a clergyman, and after the dance she confesses to 'a strong inclination for continuing the acquaintance' with him.

Mrs Allen then recognises a Mrs Thorpe with whom she had been at school. Mrs Thorpe is devoted to her children and inclined to boast about them: John being at Oxford; Edward at Merchant Taylors' School and William at sea. At the end of chapter four of *Northanger Abbey* Jane, in her characteristically witty way, decides to spare her reader an account of the 'past adventures and sufferings' of Mrs Thorpe, 'which otherwise might be expected to occupy the three or four following chapters . . .'.

Catherine makes friends with Mrs Thorpe's daughter Isabella, who is four years older than she, and Jane uses a conversation between the two of them to poke fun at the current obsession with the Gothic novel. Such novels reached their apotheosis in the works of that popular author of the day Mrs Ann Radcliffe (whose real life name Jane does not hesitate to use). When Isabella asks Catherine how she is enjoying Mrs Radcliffe's *Mysteries of Udolpho*, the latter replies that she has got as far as 'the black veil', but is intrigued to know 'what lies behind the veil'. 'Do not tell me', Catherine implores Isabella (who has already read the book):

> I would not be told upon any account. I know it must be a skeleton; I am sure it is Laurentina's skeleton [i.e. that of Mme Laurentini, a villainous character in *Mysteries of Udolpho*]. Oh! I am delighted with the book! I should like to spend my whole life reading it.

This, of course, is Jane being sarcastic about the generally syco-phantic attitude of the general public to this current genre of literature.

Catherine is displeased at the ill manners of Isabella's brother John, when he declared that his younger sisters 'looked very ugly'. John makes matters worse when, during a dance with Catherine, he bores her to tears by talking incessantly 'of the horses and dogs of the friend whom he had just left, and of the proposed exchange of terriers between them . . .' Matters do not improve for Catherine when John takes her for a drive in his carriage. She finds him:

> insufferably vain; his equipage was altogether the most com-plete of its kind in England, his carriage the neatest, his horse the best goer, and himself the best coachman.

John is equally boastful about his riding and shooting abilities.

Catherine is reunited with Henry Tilney, whom she had met at the ball, when he, his sister Eleanor and their father General Tilney, invite her to go out walking with them. However, when they fail to arrive at the allotted time, John Allen deceives her by saying that he has seen Henry Tilney out driving in a phae-ton with a 'smart-looking girl'. John has lied because he wishes Catherine to go out with him instead. 'How could you deceive me so . . .?' she asks him. Catherine is a person who keeps her word, and she expects others to do likewise.

When Eleanor Tilney asks Catherine if she is fond of history, the reply is:

> I read it a little as a duty, but it tells me nothing that does not either vex or weary me. The quarrels with popes or kings, the wars or pestilences, in every page; the men all so good for nothing, and hardly any women at all – it is very tiresome . . .

The implication is that Catherine prefers something far more exciting. Eleanor, nevertheless, declares that she herself is fond of history.

Catherine has a brother James who becomes engaged to Isabella Thorpe, but Catherine is perplexed when, at a dance, she sees Isabella (who has previously stated that she is determined *not* to dance in the absence of her fiancé) dancing with Henry's brother Captain Tilney. 'I cannot think how it can happen!' she says. Again, this is an indication that Catherine expects people to be true to their word and finds it disconcerting when they fail to be so.

Having fended off several unsuitable admirers, Catherine finally settles for Henry Tilney. She is invited to the Tilney family home – Northanger Abbey – situated some 30 miles from Bath. This brings out all the romanticism in her. She relishes the prospect and 'could not entirely subdue the hope of [discovering] some traditional legends, some awful memorials of an injured and ill-fated nun'. In other words, she wishes to experience something akin to what Mrs Radcliffe describes in her Gothic novels.

Henry adds to the tension when, on the journey, he asks Catherine if she is prepared to encounter all the horrors that a building such as 'what one reads about [in Gothic novels]' may produce?

Was she aware that the housekeeper Dorothy would show her to 'an apartment never used since some cousin or kin died in it about twenty years before'? How would she react when Dorothy gave her reason to suppose that the part of the abbey in which she lodged was, undoubtedly, haunted? And how would she feel when she discovered, 'with increased alarm', that the door of her apartment had no lock on it? When Catherine duly arrives at Northanger Abbey and settles into her apartment she is full of anticipation.

She notices in a recess on one side of the fireplace, 'an immense heavy chest'. 'What can it hold?' she asks herself and, 'Why should it be placed here?' As she examines it, 'her fearful curiosity was every moment growing greater . . .' Finally, 'her resolute effort threw back the lid', and what did she find? Merely a cotton counterpane! This is Jane, having raised her readers' expectations to a pitch – a device used commonly in the Gothic novel – bringing them suddenly back down to earth with a bump.

Not to be deterred, Catherine investigates a black cabinet with a secret drawer into which a roll of papers has been pushed, 'apparently for concealment'. Her feelings at that moment 'were indescribable. Her heart fluttered, her knees trembled, and her cheeks grew pale'. However, before she can investigate further, there is a storm and she decides to retire to bed. The following day she examines the papers, only to discover that instead of this being an ancient manuscript, such as she had hoped for, it is simply a laundry bill, tendered for the washing of shirts, stockings, cravats and waistcoats, together with another bill from a farrier 'to poultice [apply a warm dressing in order to reduce inflammation] [a] chestnut mare'. Catherine now realises how foolish she has been:

> Nothing could now be clearer [to her] than the absurdity of her recent fancy. . . . Heaven forbid that Henry Tilney should ever know her folly!

But she still has some way to go before such 'fancies' are entirely dispelled.

When General Tilney, a widower, excuses himself from going on his late wife's favourite walk, Catherine becomes suspicious of him, and even more so when he removes a portrait of her from the drawing room, on the grounds that he is dissatisfied with it. When the General shows Catherine over Northanger Abbey, and she notices that he omits to open certain doors, the tension mounts. Not only that, but when his daughter attempts to open the doors to her late mother's bedroom, he stops her. This leads Catherine to jump to the conclusion that the General had been cruel to his wife during her lifetime, and that he was now concealing something. When Catherine learns that the General would often pace the drawing room for an hour at a time, 'in silent thoughtfulness', she feels that this too 'boded nothing good'. She decides to investigate for herself, but opens the door to Henry Tilney's bedroom by mistake.

When Henry realises that Catherine suspects his father, the General, of having murdered his mother, he tells her that she has 'erred in supposing him [the General] not [to be] attached to his wife, when in fact, he loved her'. Catherine realises that her feelings had been:

> . . . all a voluntary, self-created delusion, each trifling circumstance receiving importance from an imagination resolved on alarm, and everything forced to bend to one purpose by a mind which, before she entered the Abbey, had been craving to be frightened.

Catherine becomes totally disillusioned with Mrs Radcliffe's novels portraying vice, horror, murder, slavery and poisoning. They might be appropriate for the continent of Europe, she decides, but they definitely were not appropriate for England. For had not Henry Tilney told her, 'Remember that we are English, that we are Christians'?

Catherine's thoughts turn to Isabella Thorpe. She cannot understand why Isabella, whom she previously considered to be a friend, has failed to write to her, even though she repeatedly promised to do so. Catherine finally concludes that Isabella is 'a vain coquette' whom she believes never had any regard for her, nor for her (Catherine's) brother James, with whom she had broken off an engagement in the hope of finding somebody richer and more aristocratic.

When General Tilney finally ejects Catherine from Northanger Abbey, it is not on account of her inquisitiveness. It is because, having seen her as a prospective bride for his son Henry, he had subsequently discovered that she was 'less rich than he had supposed her to be' – something which was entirely unacceptable for a prospective daughter-in-law of his. Nevertheless, Henry proposes to Catherine and she accepts him. Finally, all ends happily when the General relents and gives his consent for the couple to marry, but only after learning that Catherine is to have the sum of £3,000.

Northanger Abbey is a cautionary tale about an impressionable young lady who allows her imagination to get the better of her. This is largely because she has read too many Gothic novels – of the type which Jane Austen clearly considered to be absurd and ridiculous. Does this mean that Jane herself was lacking in romantic feelings? By no means, as the tears she shed for the loss of her lover Tom Lefroy, clearly demonstrate. Also, let it be remembered that at the conclusion of *Northanger Abbey*, her heroine Catherine Morland succeeds in marrying her knight in shining armour, Henry Tilney.

Having thoroughly debunked the Gothic novel in *Northanger Abbey*, the question became, what kind of novel would Jane write next?

❧ 13 ❧

More about the Family:
The Austens Leave Steventon

In early January 1799, Jane told Cassandra how, at the Kempshott Ball (at Kempshott Park near Basingstoke – home of the Crooke family) she had stayed overnight; Martha Lloyd kindly making room for her in her bed, where the two had lain awake and talked until 2 o'clock in the morning. Jane said, 'I love Martha better than ever . . .'[1] Despite these words, it is obvious that Jane missed her sister greatly, for later in January she tells Cassandra, 'I shall be very glad to see you home again . . .'[2] Alas for Jane, it would be another two months before the pair were reunited.

In May 1799 Jane's brother Edward decided to pay a visit to Bath for health reasons, along with his wife and children. Bath's naturally occurring thermal springs had been discovered by the Romans who had created a settlement there, known as *Aquae Sulis*. In the eighteenth century the city was transformed by architects Messrs. John Wood the elder and the younger, and Richard 'Beau' Nash. They laid out Queen Square, The Royal Crescent, the parades and The Circus – all built in the neo-classical style together with beautiful parks and gardens. The city became a magnet for royalty, the nobility, the gentry, and the new, moneyed, industrial classes. Also, those suffering from arthritis and other diseases were attracted to Bath by the spa water which was said to have healing properties. The water could either be drunk or bathed in, there being several baths including Hot Bath, King's Bath and Cross Bath. In Jane

Austen's time, the population of the city was about 30,000. Jane and her mother accompanied Edward to Bath, arriving there on 17 May and taking lodgings at 13 Queen Square. Here they stayed until 27 June.

Meanwhile, on 29 October 1799, Jane's cousin Eliza – now Mrs Henry Austen – indicated that her zest for the high life may be beginning to pall, but she had:

> not found it possible to persevere in my plan of shunning all
> society, to which I must honestly confess that I greatly prefer
> my Books, my Harp & my Pianoforte.[3]

In 1800 Revd George Austen, who was now in his 70th year, decided to retire as Rector of the Steventon and Deane parishes. From October 1800 until February 1801, Cassandra enjoyed another prolonged stay at Godmersham Park. Jane missed her sister's company and, once again, it was Martha Lloyd who filled the gap. On 1 November 1800, Jane told Cassandra that Francis had again written to her, this time to describe his adventures with the Egyptian squadron 'off the Isle of Cyprus'.[4] She also told Cassandra that she had been reading *Les Veillées du Chateau* by French writer, educator and moralist Madame de Glenlis, who was best known for her children's books.

When on 30 November Jane Austen's mother informed her that the family was intending to relocate to Bath, Jane was 'greatly distressed'.[5] In early January 1801 Jane expressed her irritation at the way in which her parents were giving away the family heirlooms and possessions to her various siblings, seemingly without discussion, prior to moving house. To Cassandra she said:

> As to our Pictures, the Battlepeice [*sic*] (a battle scene), Mr
> Nibbs, Sir Wm East, & all the old heterogeneous, miscellany,

manuscript, Scriptoral pieces dispersed over the House are to be given to James ... My Mother says that the French agricultural Prints in the best bed-room were given by Edward to his two Sisters. Do you or he know anything about it?[6]

Likewise, Jane observed that 'the brown Mare, which as well as the black was to devolve on James at our removal', had already settled herself at Deane, '& everything else I suppose will be seized by degrees in the same manner'.[7] (Jane draws a parallel between her brother James and his wife Mary's miserliness in her novel *Sense and Sensibility*).

On 24 January 1801 Henry resigned his commission and set himself up as a banker in London. In that month Jane expressed the hope that, 'Charles may, perhaps, become 1st [Lieutenant] of the [frigate] Endymion ...'[8] In May, she jubilantly reported that the *Endymion* had arrived at Portsmouth, which meant that she would see Charles very shortly. She had received a letter from him saying that he had:

received 30£ for his share of the [French] privateer [La Furie] & expects 10£ more – but of what avail is it to take prizes if he lays out the produce in presents to his Sisters. He has been buying Gold chains & topaz Crosses for us; he must be well scolded.[9]

(Charles's experience in capturing a privateer was mirrored by Jane in her novel *Persuasion*, when Captain Wentworth also made 'successive captures' of prizes).

On 4 May 1801 Jane and her mother arrived in Bath where they stayed with Mrs Austen's brother James Leigh-Perrot and his wife Jane in order to go house-hunting. A month later they were joined by the Revd Austen and Cassandra.

In October 1801 the Austens moved to 4 Sydney Place, Bath. Jane's eldest brother, the Revd James Austen, now transferred to Steventon Rectory with his second wife Mary Lloyd as curate of the parish. (James became Rector of Steventon in 1805). On the 9th of that month, Hastings de Feuillide, Eliza's son, who had been plagued by chronic illness during his short life, died.

Following their removal from Steventon to Bath, the Austens' possessions were auctioned and the notice of sale of the 'Valuable Effects at Steventon Parsonage' made for depressing reading. Included were:

[a] well made Chariot . . . and Harness, 200 volumes of books, Stump of Hay, Fowling Pieces, three Norman cows & Calves, one Horse, and other effects.

The furniture comprises four-post and field bedsteads, with dimity, moreen and other furnitures, fine feather beds and bedding, mattresses, pier and dressing glasses, floor and bedside carpets, handsome mahogany sideboard, modern set of circular dining tables on pillar and claws, Pembroke and card ditto, bureaus, chests of drawers and chairs, a piano forte in handsome case (by Ganer), a large collection of music by the most celebrated composers, an 18-inch terrestrial globe (by Adams), and microscope, mahogany library table with drawers, bookcase with six doors, eight feet by eight feet; a smaller ditto, tea china, a table set of Wedgwood ware, eight day clock, side of bacon, kitchen, dairy and brewing utensils, 13 ironbound casks, an end of hops, set of theatrical scenes &c. &c.

Later that year, a separate sale was held to dispose of the Revd Austen's farm stock and farm implements. They included:

. . . five capital cart horses, three sows, 22 pigs, and seven stores, three market waggons, two four-inch wheel dung-carts, two

narrow wheel ditto, one grass cart, four ploughs, eight har-
rows, two drags, two rollers, troughs, timber bob, shovels,
prongs, useful plough timber and iron, &c. [together with] All
the Valuable Live and Dead FARMING-STOCK, and Fine
Meadow Hay Rick, about Ten Tons. . . .'[10]

By word of explanation, 'volumes of books' may mean sets,
as Jane estimated her father's collection to number 'above
500 volumes'; the books were valued at £70; Norman cows
originate from La Manche, Normandy, France; the pianoforte
referred to was Jane's – its manufacturer being Christopher
Ganer who came to London from Leipzig in 1774. It sold for
a mere 8 guineas; the globe was made by Dudley Adams, a
mathematical instrument maker of Fleet Street; the 'theatrical
scenes' were those which the younger Austens used in their
theatrical performances.

Following the sale of their household effects, Jane wrote
bitterly about her sister-in-law: 'Mary is more minute in her
account of her own gains than in ours,'[11] implying that James's
wife was of a mercenary nature. She follows this up on 21/22
May 1801 with, 'The whole world is in a conspiracy, to enrich
one part of our family at the expense of another.'[12]

✣ 14 ✣

Romance on the Devonshire Coast: A Proposal of Marriage

The accounts of an alleged love affair, which Jane had while she and her family were on holiday in Devonshire in the very earliest years of the nineteenth century, are many and various. The most important of these accounts, which contain vital clues as to the identity of the mystery lover whom Jane allegedly met in the summer of 1801 or 1802, are quoted below. (The word 'lover' does not, of course, imply that her relationship with the gentleman in question was anything other than platonic).

For example, Caroline Austen, daughter of James by his second wife Mary Lloyd, in a letter to her brother James E. Austen-Leigh, written *c.*1869, at the time of the compilation of his *A Memoir of Jane Austen*, states that:

> During the few years my grandfather [the Revd Austen] lived at Bath, he went in the summer with his wife and daughters to some sea-side [place]. They were in Devonshire, and in Wales – and in Devonshire an acquaintance was made with some very charming man – I never heard Aunt Cassandra speak of anyone else with such admiration – she had no doubt that a mutual attachment was in progress between him and her sister. They parted – but he made it plain that he should seek them out again – and shortly afterwards he died. My Aunt [Jane's sister Cassandra] told me this in the late years of her own life, and it was quite new to me then – but all this, being nameless

and dateless, cannot I know serve any purpose of yours [i.e. of James E. Austen-Leigh's, in his writing of his *Memoir*].[1]

In another letter which Caroline wrote, this time to Mary Leigh of Adlestrop, she gives the name of the mystery lover as 'Blackall' (having previously stated above that he was 'nameless'. She wrote:

I have no doubt that Aunt Jane was beloved of several in the course of her life and was herself very capable of loving. I wish I could give you more dates as to Mr. Blackall. All that I know is this. At Newtown Aunt Cassandra was staying with us when we made the acquaintance of a certain Mr. Henry Eldridge of the Engineers. He was very pleasing and very good looking. My Aunt was much struck with him, and I was struck by her commendation as she rarely admired anyone. Afterwards she spoke of him as one so unusually gifted with all that was agreeable, and said he had reminded her strongly of a gentleman whom they had met one Summer when they were by the sea (I think she said in Devonshire) who had seemed greatly attracted by my Aunt Jane. That when they parted (I imagine he was a visitor there also, but his family might have lived near) he was urgent to know where they would be the next summer, implying or perhaps saying that he should be there also wherever it might be. I can only say the impression left on Aunt Cassandra's mind was that he had fallen in love with Aunt Jane. Soon afterwards they heard of his death. I am sure she thought him worthy of her sister from the way she recalled his memory, and also that she did not doubt either that he would have been a successful suitor.[2]

The next source of information is a diary, kept by Jane's niece Anna (James Austen's only child by his first wife Anne Mathew, who married Benjamin Lefroy). After Anna's death, Louisa (her sixth child, who in turn married the Revd Septimus Bellas) copied some extracts from her late mother's diary into a notebook. This is referred to by R. W. Chapman as the *Bellas Manuscript*, part of which reads as follows:

> The Austens with their two daughters were once at Teignmouth, the date of that visit was not later than 1802, but besides this they were once travelling in Devonshire, moving about from place to place, and I think that tour was before they left Steventon in [May] 1801, perhaps as early as 1798 or 1799. It was while they were so travelling, according to Aunt Cassandra's account many years afterwards, that they somehow made acquaintance with a gentleman of the name of Blackall. He and Aunt Jane mutually attracted each other, and such was his charm that even Aunt Cassandra thought him worthy of her sister. They parted on the understanding that he was to come to Steventon, but instead came I know not how long after a letter from his brother to say that he was dead. There is no record of Jane's affliction [i.e. sorrow following the event], but I think this attachment must have been very deep. Aunt Cassandra herself had so warm a regard for him that some years after her sister's death, she took a good deal of trouble to find out and see again his brother.[3]

Louisa Bellas provides further information in the following notes which she made about the Austen family in her copy of Lord Brabourne's *Letters of Jane Austen*. (In 1884 Edward Knatchbull, Lord Brabourne, published his collected *Letters of Jane Austen* in two volumes. His second wife was Fanny Knight, daughter of Jane's brother Edward):

> In the summer of 1801 the father, mother and daughters made a tour in Devonshire. They went to Teignmouth, Starcross,

Sidmouth etc. I believe it was at the last named place that they made acquaintance with a young clergyman when visiting his brother, who was one of the doctors of the town. He [the young clergyman] and Jane fell in love with each other, and when the Austens left he asked to be allowed to join them again further on in their tour, and the permission was given. But instead of his arriving as expected, they received a letter announcing his death. In Aunt Cassandra's memory he lived as one of the most charming persons she had known, worthy even in her eyes, of Aunt Jane.[4]

A third contributor to the account of Jane's 1801 or 1802 summer romance was Catherine, daughter of Jane's brother Francis and wife of John Hubback, a barrister. On 1 March 1870, Catherine wrote as follows to her cousin James E. Austen-Leigh and gives the impression that Jane's sister Cassandra, was the source of her information:

If ever she [Jane] was in love it was with Dr. Blackall (I think that was the name) whom they met at some watering-place, shortly before they settled at Chawton [in July 1809]. There is no doubt she admired him extremely, and perhaps regretted parting ...

Here, Catherine appears to be confusing Dr Blackall with his brother the clergyman. She continues:

I do not think Dr. Blackall died until long afterwards. [This statement, it will be noted, differs from the previous two accounts.] If I do not mistake there were two brothers, one of whom was called Mr. Edward B – and I never heard what became of him. The other, the Dr., Aunt Cassandra met with again long afterwards when she made an excursion to the Wye in company with Uncle Charles, two of his daughters and my sister Cassandra. My cousin Cassie [Cassandra] Austen, the only survivor of that party, could I have no doubt tell when and how they met him – I only remember that my Aunt found him stout, red-faced and middle-aged – very different from their youthful hero. It must have been in [18]32 or thereabouts, and I believe he died soon afterwards.[5]

Is it possible, from the incomplete and sometimes contradictory information contained in the above accounts, to identify Jane's mysterious lover? If so, then first it is necessary to examine the clues provided by the above statements individually.

THE TIME SCALE

The various narrators give the following dates of time for the alleged meeting between Jane and her lover:

Louisa Bellas gives several possibilities – 1798–99/The summer of 1801/'They parted on the understanding that he [the lover] was to come to Steventon [which the Austens left in May 1801]'.

Catherine Hubback – 'shortly before [the Austens] settled at Chawton (in July 1809)'.

THE PLACE

Louisa Bellas – while making a tour of Devonshire/by the sea/Sidmouth in Devonshire.

Catherine Hubback – A 'watering-place' (i.e. spa or seaside resort).

Caroline Austen – Devonshire.

THE IDENTITY OF THE LOVER

Louisa Bellas – a gentleman named Blackall/'a young clergy-man'.
Catherine Hubback – 'Dr Blackall (I think that was the name).'
Caroline Austen – 'Mr Blackall'.
James E. Austen-Leigh – 'a gentleman'.

THE ORIGIN OF THE LOVER

Louisa Bellas – 'a clergyman who was visiting his brother who was one of the doctors of the town'.
Caroline Austen – 'I imagine he was a visitor there [to Devonshire] . . . but his family might have lived near'.

THE FATE OF THE LOVER

Louisa Bellas – 'They parted on the understanding that he [the lover] was to come to Steventon, but instead came I know not how long after a letter from his brother to say that he was dead'./'. . . when the Austens left he asked to be allowed to join them further on in their tour . . . but instead of his arriving as expected, they received a letter announcing his death'.
Caroline Austen – 'soon afterwards [i.e. after their meeting] they heard of his [the lover's] death'./'Shortly afterwards [i.e. after their meeting] he died.'
James E. Austen-Leigh – 'within a short time [of Jane and her lover having met] they [the Austens] heard of his sudden death'.

CONCLUSION

From the above accounts there seems to be little doubt that one summer in south Devonshire, Jane met, and fell in love with a gentleman who was probably a clergyman (and who may have had a brother who was a doctor in the area). Also, from Louisa Bellas' account, it appears that her mother (James's daughter Anna) had learned, at first hand, from Cassandra that this person's name was 'Blackall'.

None of Jane's letters survive between the time she wrote to Cassandra on 26/27 May 1801 (when she was aged 25) up until 14 September 1804 (when she was aged 28), so it is difficult to be sure of her movements during this period. However, in a letter to her sister dated 8/9 January 1801, Jane states that, 'Sidmouth is now talked about as our Summer abode'. In other words, that resort on the south Devonshire coast was where the family were to spend the summer of that year. Another clue is that in August 1814 Jane wrote to her brother James's daughter Anna Austen, describing how she had visited the library at the Devonshire seaside resort of Dawlish '12 years ago' – i.e. in 1802.[6]

Jane's letters contain no other reference to Devonshire seaside resorts (Lyme Regis, which she visited in 1803 and 1804, being in Dorsetshire). It seems reasonable to suppose, therefore, that the meeting of Jane and her lover took place in the summer of either 1801 or 1802.

R.W. Chapman correctly states that the Blackalls were a West Country family.[7] However, he believes that the mention of the name 'Blackall' (by Caroline Austen and by Catherine Hubback), 'is probably a mere error'. In any case, Chapman affirms that this could not be a reference to the Revd Samuel Blackall whom Jane met in 1798, as that gentleman had not died young; in fact he 'had lived and prospered'.

Suppose for a moment that Chapman was mistaken in his first proposition, and that Jane's Devonshire lover's name was, indeed, Blackall. Suppose also, that Louisa Bellas was correct in saying that the brother of the lover was a doctor. The question then arises, was there a Dr Blackall resident in a town (Louisa Bellas' words) in South Devonshire, probably on or near the coast at the requisite time? The answer is yes.

John Blackall MD (1772–1860) was the 6th son of the Revd Theophilus Blackall – a prebendary of Exeter Cathedral – and his wife Anne (*née* Drewe), and the great-grandson of Offspring Blackall, Bishop of Exeter. In June 1797 John was appointed physician to the Devon and Exeter Hospital in Exeter, Devonshire's county town. In 1798 he relocated to the south Devonshire town of Totnes (5 miles inland from the coastal town of Paignton and 12 miles inland from the coastal town of Teignmouth)[8], 'where he became physician to the district'.[9] Here he remained until 1806, when he returned to take up his former post at Exeter.

The next question is, did Dr John Blackall have a brother who was a clergyman? Again, the answer is yes. In fact, John had three surviving brothers. Of these, Henry (1769–1845) was a magistrate, a Sheriff and also Mayor of Exeter on a number of occasions, and Thomas (1773–1821) was the Vicar of Tardebigge in Worcestershire. The great surprise is that John had a third surviving brother Samuel – baptised on 6 December 1770 – who was two years his senior.[10] The year of Samuel's birth, 1770, correlates precisely with that of the Revd Samuel Blackall, whom Jane had met in 1798. Also, William Austen-Leigh confirms the fact that one of Samuel's brothers was 'John Blackall, of Balliol College, Oxford, for many years a distinguished Exeter physician'.[11] (In fact, John was BA, MA, MB and MD of Balliol College, Oxford. It should be noted that in the Blackall family tree, provided by the Society of Genealogists, there is no mention of an Edward Blackall, so from where Catherine Hubback obtained this name is not known).

A possible explanation for the sequence of events which led to the meeting between Jane and the Revd Samuel Blackall in South Devonshire in the summer of 1802, after an interval of three and a half years, is now given. Blackall, probably through Mrs Lefroy, learned that the Austens were holidaying in South Devon. He had already stated in 1798 that it would give him 'particular pleasure to have the opportunity of improving my acquaintance with that family – with a hope of creating to myself a nearer interest'. Now that the opportunity had presented itself, he would go to stay with his brother Dr John Blackall at Totnes, and hope to meet the Austens during the course of his stay.

As for the Austens, it is quite possible that they were aware that Samuel had a brother in Totnes; that this brother Dr John Blackall was a man of considerable reputation, 'famed for his skill in diagnosis',[12] and that his particular speciality was in the treatment of dropsy (oedema). Here it should also be noted that Jane, in a letter to her sister Cassandra dated 18 December 1798, includes 'dropsy' [oedema] and 'water in her chest' as two of her mother's principal complaints. So what could be more natural than for Mrs Cassandra Austen to seek Dr John Blackall out in order to consult him?

The above accounts by Caroline Austen and Louisa Bellas give rise to further questions. Both believed that soon after his meeting with Jane, her lover (the Revd Samuel Blackall) died. And yet, it is a fact that Blackall lived on to the year 1842, when he died at the age of 72. How can this be explained?

Close examination of Caroline Austen's and Louisa Bellas' statements, as given above, reveals that in both cases their information was based, directly or indirectly, upon information supplied to them by Jane's sister Cassandra in the latter's declining years. Bearing in mind that Cassandra took it upon herself to destroy many of Jane's letters after her death, had she deliberately put out false information about the fate of the gentleman whose name she admitted was Blackall? If so, what was her motive for doing so? Was it because she wished to save the Revd Samuel Blackall – who had married long since – from any embarrassment? If so, then this was quite understandable. Or was there another explanation – one which had more to do with Cassandra's own reputation? This will be discussed shortly.

Another question arises from the account of Catherine Hubback, who relates Cassandra's excursion to the Wye in the company of four other members of the Austen family, with the purpose of meeting up with Jane's mystery lover's brother, the doctor. The Wye presumably means the River Wye, of which there are three. One passes through the counties of Cardiganshire, Montgomeryshire, Radnorshire, Herefordshire, Gloucestershire and Monmouthshire; one through Buckinghamshire, and one through Derbyshire. Whichever River Wye it was, it does not correlate with the fact that Dr John Blackall lived out his life in Devonshire, practised in Exeter and finally died in that city in January 1860. Or could it be that Samuel had another brother, apart from John, who was also a doctor? The previously mentioned Blackall family tree indicates that this was not the case. Therefore, the identity of the gentleman from the Wye remains a mystery.

Assuming that Jane and Samuel were reunited in the summer of 1802, why did their relationship not prosper? Perhaps this was for the same reason that it had failed to prosper when the couple had first met in 1798; mainly that Samuel simply could not afford to support a wife. Or was there another reason; one which related to Jane's sister Cassandra? Again, this will be discussed shortly.

On 25 March 1802 the Treaty of Amiens brought the war with France to a close. It was probably after this that Henry Austen resigned his commission and moved to London, to Upper Berkeley Street with his family. Here, he set up as a banker with offices in Cleveland Court, St James.

December 1802 found Jane staying with the Bigg-Withers family at Manydown Park, Wootton St Lawrence, Hampshire. When the wealthy young Harris Bigg-Wither (who was six years Jane's junior and whose sisters were Jane and Cassandra's childhood friends) made Jane a proposal of marriage, she accepted. However, by the following morning she had had second thoughts and decided to retract, whereupon both she and Cassandra immediately returned to Bath. Catherine Hubback said, 'It was in a momentary fit of self-delusions that she [Aunt Jane] accepted Mr Withers' proposal . . .'[13]

From a letter which Jane wrote subsequently to Cassandra, it is known that she was in Lyme Regis on the Dorsetshire coast (referred to by Jane simply as 'Lyme'; it received its Royal Charter in 1284) on 5 November 1803, when she witnessed a large fire which had broken out in the town.[14]

Lyme Regis is famous for its stone-built cobb which juts out into Lyme Bay to form an artificial harbour. The town became popular with visitors from about 1775 onwards, when coaches ran directly between that town and the city of Bath. Lyme Regis's Assembly Rooms were built in about 1775, near to which bathing machines (mobile changing rooms) were available. Sea-bathing became even more popular when King George III visited Weymouth, another of Dorset's seaside towns; the first occasion being in 1789. In Jane Austen's time, Lyme Regis boasted several hotels; the most fashionable being the 'Three Cups'.[15] Jane was extremely fond of Lyme Regis, and one day it would feature in one of her novels.

Following the resumption of the war between Britain and France on 18 May 1803 after a brief truce, Francis was ordered to command the 'Sea Fencibles' – a volunteer force whose duty it was to prevent an enemy landing on the coast of southern England. To this end, he took up residence in Ramsgate, Kent, where Jane duly visited him that autumn. The war would continue for another twelve years.

September 1804 found the Austens once again at Lyme Regis in company with Jane's brother Henry and his wife Eliza, staying at Pyne House, Broad Street. From here, Henry and Cassandra subsequently went to Weymouth, while Jane and her parents remained in Lyme Regis at a small boarding house in the town. For Jane, the sea always had a strong, romantic attachment and she may have been thinking of Lyme Regis when, in *Sanditon*, her character Sir Edward Denham describes 'the terrific grandeur of the ocean in a storm, its glassy surface in a calm, its gulls and its samphire . . .'

And yet Jane was aware of its dangers, for Denham goes on to say:

> . . . and the deep fathoms of its abysses, its quick vicissitudes, its direful deceptions, its mariners tempting it in sunshine and overwhelmed by the sudden tempest . . .[16]

By the time the Austens returned to Bath that autumn, the lease had expired on Sydney Place; they therefore relocated to Green Park Buildings.

❧ 15 ❧

The Watsons

During her time in Bath, Jane's writing of novels came to a virtual standstill, possibly because the fullness of her social life left her precious little time for this pastime, and also because she had been uprooted from her beloved Steventon to a place in which she did not feel entirely happy. However, according to Fanny Lefroy, her brother James's granddaughter, one novel which Jane did commence in Bath, 'somewhere in 1804', was *The Watsons*.[1] The work was left unfinished, possibly because of the death of her father on 21 January 1805. (In fact, *The Watsons* was not published until 1871 by James E. Austen-Leigh, who included it in his *A Memoir of Jane Austen*).

The Watsons are described as a poor family who live in Surrey and have 'no close [enclosed] carriage'. Emma Watson has recently returned to the family having been brought up by an aunt. She has a brother Robert of Croydon, whose wife Jane she despises for her narrow-mindedness.

Emma's elder sister Elizabeth describes herself as having been ill-used. She had been attached to a man by the name of Purvis, however, another of her sisters, Penelope, whom she had trusted had 'set him against me, with a view of gaining him herself'. Such treachery, says Elizabeth, 'has been the ruin of my happiness. I shall never love any man as I loved Purvis'.

'Could a sister do such a thing?' asks the incredulous Emma.

'[D]o not trust her,' says Elizabeth, 'she has her good qualities, but she has no faith, no honour, no scruples, if she can promote her own advantage'.

A ball is to be held at the White Hart Inn by the Edwards who are 'people of fortune' and who live in the 'best house in the street'. Emma is to attend, but before she does so, her more experienced sister Elizabeth cautions her against a certain Tom Musgrave who, although he has 'about eight or nine hundred pounds a year', is 'a great flirt and never means anything serious'. Nonetheless, Elizabeth stresses how important it is that she and her sisters marry as their father cannot provide for them, 'and it is very bad to grow old and be poor and laughed at'. Penelope, says Elizabeth, is currently attempting 'to make some match at Chichester [with] rich old Dr Harding'. Another sister, Margaret, described as 'all gentleness and mildness ... if a little fretful and perverse', believes erroneously that Tom Musgrave is seriously in love with her. As for Emma's brothers, Robert 'has got a good wife and six thousand pounds', whereas Sam is 'only a surgeon'.

The ball is attended by a Captain Hunter (whose brother officer asks Emma to dance); Lady Osborne of Osborne Castle and her son Lord Osborne and daughter Miss Osborne; Mr Howard, 'formerly tutor to Lord Osborne, now clergyman of the parish in which the castle stood'. Howard is described as 'an agreable-looking [sic] man, a little more than thirty'. In contrast, Lord Osborne is 'not fond of women's company' and does not dance.

After the ball, when Emma is expecting her father's 'chair' (conveyance) to take her home, Tom Musgrave appears bearing a note from her sister Elizabeth. This is to say that it is impossible for Emma to return home until the following morning because her father has decided to go out in the conveyance himself in order to attend a 'visitation' (a visit to the parish by an ecclesiastical superior).

When Tom offers to take her home instead, Emma declines his offer. This is because she finds him to be 'very vain, very conceited, absurdly anxious for distinction, and absolutely contemptible in some of the measures he takes for becoming so'. The Revd Howard's manners, on the other hand, are 'of a kind to give me much more ease and confidence'. Emma therefore avails herself of her hostess Mrs Edwards' invitation to stay overnight.

When Emma does finally return home, she hears her father describing the visitation which he had attended where Howard, who was the preacher, had 'given an excellent sermon'. Mr Watson was also impressed by the way Howard had helped him up a steep flight of steps when he was suffering with his, 'gouty foot'.

When Lord Osborne and Tom Musgrave pay the Watsons an unexpected visit, Emma finds the occasion embarrassing, bearing in mind the 'very humble style' in which she and her family were obliged to live, in contrast to 'the elegancies of life' which she had previously enjoyed with her aunt.

Jane Austen's unfinished novel *The Watsons* is a story with many themes: Emma's ability to differentiate between the superior qualities of Mr Howard, as compared with Lord Osborne and Tom Musgrave; plus her ability to recognise the materialistic nature of her brother Robert, who was more intent on:

> ... pondering over a doubtful halfcrown, than on welcoming a sister who was no longer likely to have any property for him to get the direction [possession] of.

Emma was also painfully aware of the condescending attitude of Robert's wife. Were there allusions here to Jane's eldest brother James and his wife Mary, who seemed anxious to lay their hands on as many of the Austen possessions as possible, at the time of the family's removal from Steventon to Bath? However, she delighted in the companionship of her father who, 'being a man of sense and education, was if able, to converse, a welcome companion', and who even though he was ill made few demands other than to receive 'gentleness and silence'.

The most significant theme in *The Watsons* is that of the rivalry between sisters Elizabeth and Penelope, as they vie with one another for a partner. In no other work by Jane is her language so blunt, so outspoken, so censorious, so bitter, as when she describes the treacherousness displayed by Penelope to Elizabeth over Elizabeth's lover Purvis. Why should this be so? Why had Jane, on this unique occasion, abandoned her normally moderate tone and launched into a full-scale attack on Penelope? Did this reaction by Jane stem from some bitter hurt which she herself had sustained? If so, was it at the hands of her own sister Cassandra? When writing of Penelope, was it really Cassandra whom Jane had in mind?

This theory might appear fanciful, were it not for the following poem, written by Jane and discovered by Lord Brabourne, 'enclosed in one of the [i.e. Jane's] Letters of 1807' (the poem was probably written in that year, but may have been written earlier):

'Miss Austen' (Cassandra)

Love, they say, is like a rose;
I'm sure 'tis like the wind that blows,
For not a human creature knows
How it comes or where it goes.

It is the cause of many woes:
It swells the eyes and reds the nose,
And very often changes those
Who once were friends to bitter foes.

From its title there is no doubt that the sentiments expressed are addressed by Jane to her sister. There is also no doubt that it is the last line which is the most significant. But who were these bitter foes? Or was Jane speaking in general terms about human attachments? But if so, why choose such a painful subject to dwell upon? Or could it be that Jane and Cassandra, as a result of a love affair, had themselves become 'bitter foes'? Is it possible, therefore, that in both her novel *The Watsons*, and in her poem 'Miss Austen', Jane was expressing her disapproval, as strongly as she knew how, of the fact that her sister Cassandra had attempted to steal her gentleman friend?

Nonetheless, in the latter part of the poem a reconciliation is proposed:

But let us now the scene transpose
And think no more of tears and throes.
Why may we not as well suppose
A smiling face the urchin shows?
And when with joy the bosom glows,
And when the heart had full repose,
'Tis mutual love the gift bestows.[2]

Did reconciliation subsequently occur between Jane and Cassandra, and was this a factor in Jane being able to regain her composure to the extent that she was eventually able to resume her novel writing?

If the sisters did fall out over a lover, who might this lover have been?

TOM LEFROY

Lefroy is an unlikely candidate, the reason for his break-up from Jane being that he was recalled to Ireland by his family. Also, at the time of Tom and Jane's association in late 1795, Cassandra was engaged to the Revd Thomas Fowle.

HARRIS BIGG-WITHER

Bigg-Wither is alleged to have proposed marriage to Jane in December 1802. However, something of a smokescreen has been cast over this event. Between May 1801 and January 1805, no letters of Jane's survive (with the exception of one she wrote to Cassandra in September 1804). This is either because during this 'missing letter' phase, no letters were written, which seems unlikely, or because Cassandra deliberately destroyed them after Jane's death. Also, Caroline Austen told her brother James E. Austen-Leigh: 'My own wish would be, that not any allusion should be made to the Manydown story [i.e. of Harris's alleged proposal.]'[3]

The Bigg-Wither episode occurred during the 'missing letter' phase, and therefore Harris cannot entirely be ruled out as object of Jane and Cassandra's supposed rivalry – even if no blame attaches to him for it. (Harris, like Purvis in *The Watsons*, was married soon after his break-up with Jane, in November 1804, to Anne Frith). Catherine Hubback made light of the event: 'I think the affair vexed her [Jane] a good deal, but I am sure she had no attachment for him [Bigg-Wither]'.[4]

Jane by her sister Cassandra. (Private collection)

Left: The author with Mrs Diana Shervington, Ambassador Hotel, Lyme Regis, 10 July 2008.

Below left: The Reverend George Austen as a young man. (Courtesy of Jane Austen Memorial Trust)

Below right: Mrs Austen. (Courtesy of Jane Austen Memorial Trust)

Steventon Rectory (Parsonage); wood engraving used in J.E. Austen-Leigh's *A Memoir of Jane Austen*, 1870.

Steventon Rectory, Jane's birthplace, 1814; rear view by Anna Lefroy. (Courtesy of Jane Austen Memorial Trust)

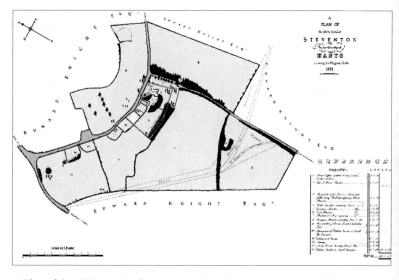

A Plan of the Glebe Land of Steventon, 1821. (Hampshire Record Office)

KEY: 1. Steventon Rectory, yard, farm buildings, barns, part of kitchen garden and lawns; 2. Part of home meadow; 3. Lawn and shrubbery; 4. South meadow; 5. Quintence meadow; 6. East meadow; 7. Plantation; 8. Hanging meadow; 9. Remainder of home meadow; 10. Remainder of kitchen garden; 11. Cottage and garden; 12. Nursery; 13. Nursery meadow; 14. Cottage garden and small plantation.

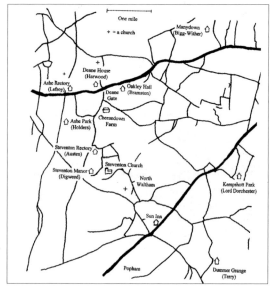

Steventon and district.

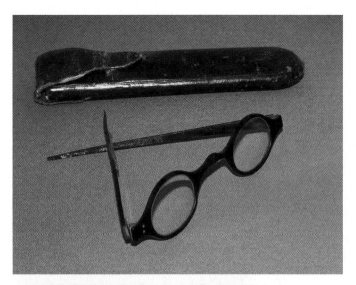

Above: Mrs Austen's spectacles and case. (Courtesy of Mrs Diana Shervington)

Left: Ivory sticks for 'spillikins', letter counters, and fish (the purpose for which is unknown) all from Steventon Rectory. (Courtesy of Mrs Diana Shervington)

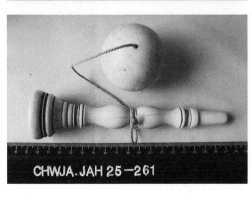

Below left: Cup and ball which belonged to Jane. (Courtesy of Jane Austen Memorial Trust)

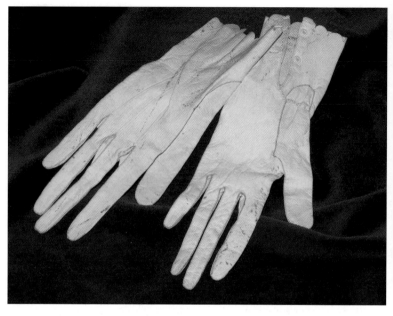

Jane's kid gloves. (Courtesy of Mrs Diana Shervington)

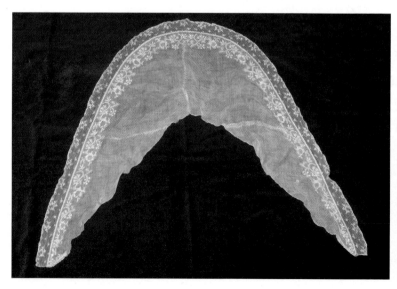

Jane's lace collar. (Courtesy of Mrs Diana Shervington)

Jane's cap for indoor use, decorated with lace, from Steventon Rectory. (Courtesy of Mrs Diana Shervington)

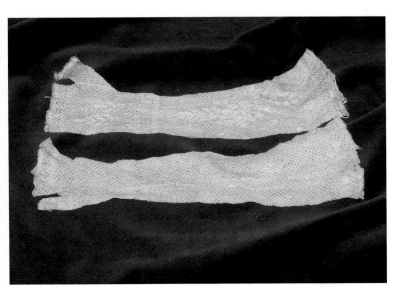

Mrs Austen's fingerless gloves. (Courtesy of Mrs Diana Shervington)

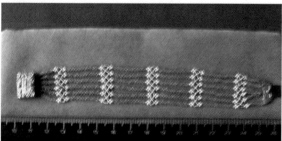

Above: Jane's sampler.

Left: A bracelet which belonged to Jane. (Courtesy of Jane Austen Memorial Trust)

Above left: Jane's sister, Cassandra Austen (silhouette). (Private Family Collection. Courtesy of Jane Austen Memorial Trust)

Above right: Eliza de Feuillide, by an unknown French artist.

Left: Writing table used by Jane in the cottage at Chawton. (Courtesy of Jane Austen Memorial Trust)

A French song, copied by Jane into her music book. (Courtesy of Jane Austen Memorial Trust)

Above left: Mrs Lefroy. (Courtesy of Jane Austen Memorial Trust)

Above right: Tom Lefroy. (Courtesy of Judy and Brian Harden)

Above left: Jane Austen (silhouette). (Courtesy of Jane Austen Memorial Trust)

Above right: Jane Austen's rose cockade of egrets' feathers, which she wore to commemorate Rear Admiral Sir Horatio Nelson's defeat of the French fleet in the Battle of the Nile, 1–2 August 1798. (Courtesy of Mrs Diana Shervington)

Topaz crosses bought for Jane and her sister Cassandra by their brother Charles. (Courtesy of Jane Austen Memorial Trust)

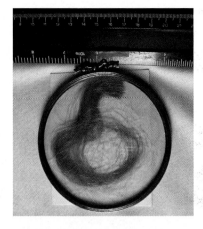

Left: Lock of Jane Austen's hair. (Courtesy of Jane Austen Memorial Trust)

Below: A quilt made by Jane, her mother and her sister. (Courtesy of Jane Austen Memorial Trust)

'The New Game of Emulation' – subtitled 'Abhorrence of Vice and a Love of Virtue' – a game which came from Chawton Cottage and which Jane undoubtedly played. (Courtesy of Ronald Bragg)

Above: Henry Austen. (Courtesy of Jane Austen Memorial Trust)

Right and below: The 'Godmersham children' – Jane's nephews and nieces (silhouette). (Courtesy of Ronald Bragg)

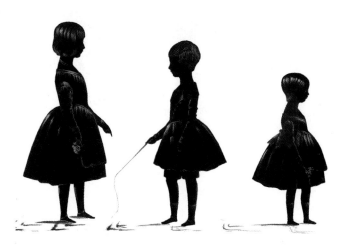

Jane Austen, 1870 (woodcut). (Courtesy of Jane Austen Memorial Trust)

THE REVD SAMUEL BLACKALL

Jane and Blackall met for the first time in the summer or early autumn of 1798. Evidence has been put forward that he reappeared briefly on the scene in the summer of 1802 when, during a visit to his brother John in Totnes, Devonshire, he was reunited with the Austens who were on holiday in the vicinity. By this time, Cassandra's fiancé the Revd Thomas Fowle, had died (February 1797) and once again, the year 1802 falls within the 'missing letter' period.

Was Jane wronged by Cassandra, and did the latter, like Penelope in *The Watsons*, attempt, in Elizabeth's words, 'to set him [in this case the Revd Blackall] against me, with a view to gaining him herself'? And if so, did this prompt Jane to express her feelings of outrage towards her sister in her subsequent letters, and was this the real reason why Cassandra deliberately destroyed so many of them?

Likewise, was this falling out between the two sisters the real reason that Jane failed to complete *The Watsons*, which had the prospect of being equally as meritorious as any novel that she had written before, and would write subsequently? Also, why was publication of *The Watsons* delayed until fifty-four years after Jane's death (and twenty-six years after the death of Cassandra)? Could the reason have been that if Jane's explosive words about Penelope's treachery towards Elizabeth had become known to Cassandra, which would inevitably have been the case, then this would have opened up a final, deep and unbridgeable rift between the two of them?

What other clues does Jane's novel *The Watsons* provide? When Elizabeth declares that 'very few people marry their first loves', this is reminiscent of the failed relationship between Jane and Tom Lefroy. However, when Elizabeth states that Purvis went on, soon after, to marry somebody else, this does not accord with what is known about either Tom Lefroy or Samuel Blackall. It is, therefore, unwise to attempt to extrapolate too rigorously the relationship between real people and the fictional characters of the novels. Nevertheless, the theme of love and treachery between sisters is a powerful one, and not easily dismissed.

On 16 December 1804, which happened to be Jane's 29th birthday, Mrs Lefroy died in a fall from her horse. Then came another blow; on 21 January 1805 Jane's father George died, whereupon she wrote:

> Our Father has closed his virtuous & happy life in a death almost as free from suffering as his Children could have wished. His tenderness as a Father, who can do justice to [it]?[5]

With the death of the Revd George Austen, his eldest son James, curate of Steventon since 1801, became its rector.

When George Austen died, so did his clergyman's pension of £600 per annum. From then on, the impecunious Austens were obliged to spend their summers with Jane's brothers Henry and Edward, and the season in Bath, where Mrs Austen could continue to enjoy the company of the Leigh-Perrots.

That Jane's relationship with Henry and his wife Eliza was a warm and enduring one is vouched for by a letter Jane wrote to Cassandra in April 1805. Henry, says Jane:

> expresses himself as greatly pleased with the Screen, & says that he does not know whether he is, 'most delighted with the idea

or the Execution.' [This implies that the screen – perhaps made to hide a fireplace or to partition a room – was made, or at least embroidered, by Jane herself.] Eliza of course, goes halves in all this, and there is also just such a message of warm acknowledgement from her respecting the Broche as you would expect.[6]

In April 1805 the Austens moved to 25 Gay Street. For their income they now depended on Jane's brothers James and Henry, each contributing an annual sum of £50, and Edward contributing an annual sum of £100. In addition, Cassandra derived a small income from the interest paid on her £1,000 inheritance from the estate of her late fiancé Thomas Fowle, and Mrs Austen had modest means of her own, amounting to about £200.

At Godmersham Park in August that year, Jane made it clear that she did not appreciate her straitened financial circumstances. However, her hairdresser Mr Hall had been considerate in charging her only 2s 6d for a haircut. 'He certainly respects either our Youth or our poverty' she remarked dryly.[7]

In view of the difficulties at that time, it might reasonably be asked why Jane did not look for employment. The answer was that her books were beginning to bring in a modest income; otherwise, she might well have become governess to the children of some wealthy family.

In October, Francis narrowly missed taking part in the Battle of Trafalgar, which took place on the 21st of that month, between the British fleet on the one hand, and the French and Spanish fleets on the other. Instead of joining the battle, his ship *Canopus* (a prize ship which was originally *Le Franklin*), which Admiral Horatio Nelson had placed under his command, was required to travel to Gibraltar to collect water and stores. Francis did, however, see action in 1806 in the Battle of Saint Domingue (Santo Domingo – a French colony until

1804, when it became independent as Haiti) in the West Indies, when his squadron captured three French prize ships. His share of the prize money allowed him to fix a date for his marriage to Mary Gibson of Ramsgate: this took place on 24 July of that year. (Francis was the fourth of Jane's brothers to marry).

Francis and Mary set up home in Southampton, the city being situated conveniently near to the naval base at Portsmouth, and in October 1806 they invited Jane, Cassandra, their mother and Martha Lloyd to join them. In January 1807 Cassandra received an invitation to Godmersham Park, where she remained until the following month. Jane was not amused. In a letter to her sister dated 8/9 February, she stated as follows:

> Frank & Mary cannot at all approve of your not being at home
> in time to help them in their finishing purchases [presumably,
> their final purchases of items for the home].

Jane also expressed regret that her sister's return was to be delayed. But she said:

> It is no use to lament – I never heard that even Queen Mary's
> lamentation [the title of a song with which Jane was familiar]
> did her any good ...

The same letter reveals just how cool the relationship between Jane and her brother James had become:

> I should not be surprised if we were to be visited by James again
> this week. . . . I am sorry & angry that his Visits should not give
> one more pleasure; the company of so good & so clever a Man
> ought to be gratifying in itself; – but his Chat seems all forced,
> his Opinions on many points too much copied from his Wife's,
> & his time here is spent I think in walking about the House &
> banging the Doors, or ringing the bell for a glass of water.[8]

On 20/22 February 1807, when Jane wrote again to Cassandra, she could scarcely conceal her annoyance with the latter, who to her way of thinking, was seldom in the right place at the right time:

> I confess myself much disappointed by the repeated delay in your return, for tho' I had pretty well given up any idea of your being with us before our removal [to Godmersham Park], I felt sure that March would not pass away without bringing you. Before April comes, of course something else will occur to detain you. But as you are happy, all this is Selfishness [i.e. on Jane's part].[9]

Meanwhile Charles, while stationed in Bermuda, had met 17-year-old Frances Fitzwilliam Palmer ('Fanny'), daughter of the island's former Attorney-General. The pair were married on 19 May 1807. In March 1808 Francis was given command of HMS *St Albans*, in which vessel he voyaged to South Africa, China and the East Indies.

On 15 June 1808 it was Jane's turn to be invited to Godmersham Park and she makes no secret of the fact that she looks forward to the luxurious life there: 'I shall eat Ice & drink French wine, & be above Vulgar Economy.'[10]

Over a week later, on 26 June, Jane tells Cassandra that, 'We are all very happy to hear of his [Francis's] health and safety', and a few days later she is exuberant at the prospect of seeing her seafaring brother again. She writes to her sister:

> I give you all Joy of Frank's return, which happens in the true Sailor way, just after our being told not to expect him for some weeks.[11]

In August, Francis found himself in command of a flotilla of ships transporting troops to Corunna, north-west Spain, in support of Sir Arthur Wellesley, Duke of Wellington, and bringing wounded English soldiers and French prisoners back to Spithead (Portsmouth). The Duke had been sent to assist the Portuguese against France in the Peninsular War.

At the end of September Cassandra made another visit to Godmersham Park; this time for Edward's wife Elizabeth's confinement with her eleventh child. Tragedy then struck because on 10 October, ten days after the birth of a boy, Brook John, Elizabeth died. Cassandra was required to remain with Edward while the latter's eldest two sons George and Edward were taken by coach from Winchester College, where they were pupils, to Southampton, to be looked after for a time by Jane. Mourning clothes were purchased for them and during that period Jane took them on several excursions up the Hamble river where they saw a naval ship under construction. In a letter to Cassandra, Jane expressed her feelings:

> . . . dearest Edward, whose loss & whose suffering seem to make those of every other person nothing. – God be praised! . . . that he has a religious Mind to bear him up, & a Disposition that will gradually lead him to comfort.[12]

Once again, Jane found herself missing her sister greatly. On 24/25 October she wrote to Cassandra saying, 'As to your lengthened stay, it is no more than I expected, and what must be, but you cannot suppose I like it'.[13] (In the event, Cassandra did not return to Southampton until February 1809).

On 16 December 1808, which was her birthday, Jane composed a poem in memory of Mrs Lefroy who had died exactly four years previously:

> Beloved friend, four years have pass'd away
> Since thou wert snatch'd forever from our eyes

However much she regretted the fact that Mrs Lefroy had been instrumental in sending away her nephew and lover Tom, Jane had clearly forgiven her.

Jane's letters indicate that she made frequent visits to Henry and Eliza at Sloane Street, and yet in that month of December 1808, she requests of Cassandra, 'Send me some intelligence of Eliza, it is a long while since I have heard of her'. A month later Jane tells Cassandra, 'Your report of Eliza's health gives me great pleasure'.[14]

In April 1809 the Austens left Southampton for Bookham in Surrey, home of Mrs Austen's cousin and namesake Cassandra Cooke (*née* Leigh), and Godmersham Park. That summer, Jane's brother Edward generously invited Jane, Cassandra, Mrs Austen and Martha Lloyd to live at Chawton Cottage in Hampshire; this was a part of the Chawton Estate which he had inherited from Thomas Knight II. They accepted and took possession of the property on 7 July.

In that month Jane sent a delightful poem, which she had written, to Francis on the birth of his and his wife Mary's son, Francis William Austen junior:

My Dearest Frank I wish you Joy
Of Mary's safety [i.e. safe delivery]
with a boy ...[15]

In the summer of 1810 Francis returned from China aboard the ship *St Albans* which was laden with gold and treasure – he being an agent of the East India Company. For transporting this precious cargo he received from the company the princely sum of £1,500.

The following spring Jane visited Eliza and Henry at Sloane Street in order that she might correct the proofs of her novel *Sense and Sensibility*, sent to her by her publisher Thomas

Egerton. Other things which Jane looked forward to included attending a party with Eliza, going for a walk with her, and also meeting her friends Comte d'Antraigues and his wife Mme St Huberti, formerly an operatic prima donna, and their son Comte Julien). 'It will be amusing to see the ways of a French circle' she says.[16]

Also around this time, on 14 October 1812, Thomas Knight II's widow Catherine died, whereupon Edward changed his name to 'Knight'.

⚜ 16 ⚜

Mansfield Park

The novel was commenced in 1811, completed in the summer of 1813, when Jane was aged 38, and published in 1814 by Thomas Egerton.

Mansfield Park, in the county of Northamptonshire, is the country seat of Sir Thomas and Lady Bertram. Lady Bertram has a sister Frances, who is married to Lieutenant Price of the Marines: a man 'without education, fortune, or connections'. Living near to Mansfield Park at the White House is another of Lady Bertram's sisters, Mrs ('Aunt') Norris, wife of a clergyman who, subsequently, becomes a widow.

When the impecunious Mrs Frances Price is expecting her ninth child, she and her husband appeal to the wealthy Bertrams, who agree to assist them by inviting their eldest daughter Fanny to live with them at Mansfield Park. Fanny, the heroine of the novel, is then 9 years old and described as:

> small of [for] her age, with no glow of complexion, nor any other striking beauty; exceedingly timid and shy, and shrinking from notice . . .

But with a sweet voice and a pretty countenance. At Mansfield Park Fanny finds a friend in Edmund, Sir Thomas Bertram's youngest son who is destined to be a clergyman. Fanny describes Edmund as someone whose 'friendship never failed her'.

Tom Bertram is Sir Thomas's eldest son and his heir. However, he lives an extravagant lifestyle and is told by Sir Thomas that as a result he has robbed his brother Edmund 'for ten, twenty, thirty years, perhaps for life, of more than half the income which ought to be his'.

Sir Thomas visits Antigua (Leeward Islands) where he has financial interests, whereupon his daughters Maria and Julia consider themselves to be 'immediately at their own disposal, and to have every indulgence within their reach'. Maria, 'who was beginning to think matrimony a duty', becomes informally engaged to Mr Rushworth of 'Sotherton'. Such a match 'would give her the enjoyment of a larger income than her father's, as well as ensure her of the house in town'.

Aunt Norris becomes a perpetual thorn in Fanny's side. In one instance she declares that it is both unnecessary and improper that she should have 'a regular lady's horse of her own in the style of her cousins'. However, she is overruled by Edmund.

A wealthy young brother and sister, Henry and Mary Crawford, come to visit Mary's half-sister Mrs Grant, wife of Dr Grant the parson. It is Mrs Grant's notion that Henry should marry the youngest Miss Bertram – Julia, whereupon Mary cautions her against it. Her brother Henry, she says, 'is the most horrible flirt that can be imagined. If your Miss Bertrams do not like to have their hearts broke, let them avoid Henry'.

Whereas Mary is a creature of the town, Fanny is a creature of the country. For example, when Mr Rushworth talks of having an avenue of trees cut down at his house 'Sotherton', Fanny expresses her regret by quoting the poet William Cowper: 'Ye fallen avenues, once more I mourn your fate unmerited'.

Mary was brought up by her uncle and guardian Admiral Crawford. On his wife's death the Admiral, who is described as 'a man of vicious conduct', makes it impossible for Mary to go on living with him at his London home because it is now occupied not only by himself, but also by his mistress. Mary decides, therefore, to make a home with the Grants at the parsonage. Speaking of the Admiral's house, where she was brought up, Mary says that 'Of Rears and Vices, I saw enough. Now, do not be suspecting me of a pun. I entreat'. Edmund considers this joke to be in poor taste, and is not impressed.

Despite Mary's faults, which are all too apparent to Fanny, Edmund finds himself falling in love with her. When Mary expresses the desire to learn to ride, Edmund offers her a mare which Fanny considers to be hers. Edmund subsequently notices that Fanny is suffering as a result of spending too much time indoors. He becomes angry with himself for having left her for 'four days together without any choice of companions or exercise'.

When Fanny has the opportunity to visit the Rushworths at 'Sotherton', Aunt Norris continues with her personal vendetta against her by declaring that it is 'quite out of the question', as Lady Bertram cannot possibly spare her. In this Edmund over-rides her once again. When Fanny is offered the east room of the house, Aunt Norris shows her spitefulness by stipulating that no warming fire would be lit in the hearth 'on Fanny's account'.

At 'Sotherton' Mr Rushworth's guests are shown the chapel, where Mary Crawford makes disparaging remarks about the church by referring to those 'poor housemaids and footmen' who are required 'to leave business and pleasure, and say their prayers here twice a day'. In her opinion, it was:

> safer to leave people to their own devices on such subjects [and] to chuse [their] own time and manner of devotion.

The amateur theatricals held at Mansfield Park are reminiscent of those organised by Jane's eldest brother James in the improvised theatre set up in the barn at Steventon. When Fanny is asked to perform a part, in a play of which she disapproves, she objects vigorously. At this Aunt Norris declares:

> I shall think her a very obstinate, ungrateful girl, if she does not do what her Aunt, and Cousins wish her – very ungrateful indeed, considering who and what she is.

Mary then attempts to comfort Fanny. (Here, Jane Austen demonstrates, once again, her belief that very few people are entirely without some redeeming features).

Edmund, who previously declared that he would not act in the play, is persuaded to do so, whereupon Fanny reprimands him saying that she is:

> sorry to see you drawn in to do what you had resolved against, and what you are known to think would be disagreeable to my uncle.

Fanny finds herself increasingly isolated:

> Every body around her was gay and busy, prosperous and important . . . She alone was sad and insignificant; she had no share in any thing; she might go or stay, she might be in the midst of their noise, or retreat from it to the solitude of the east room without being seen or missed.

Just as Fanny reluctantly succumbs to the pressure and agrees to accept a part in the play, Sir Thomas Bertram returns home. He is delighted to see her again and greets her 'with a kindness which astonished and penetrated her, calling her his dear Fanny, kissing her affectionately'.

When Sir Thomas shows his displeasure at what has been going on in his absence, Edmund admits that 'we have all been more or less to blame'. But he does admit to his father that this does not include Fanny who was

> ... the only one who has judged rightly throughout, who has been consistent. Her feelings being steadily against it from first to last. She never ceased to think of what was due to you.

Mary complains about the 'remoteness', 'unpunctuality' and 'exorbitant charges and frauds' of the local nurseryman and the poulterer, and states that she means to be 'too rich to lament or feel any thing of the sort'.

When Mrs Grant asks Fanny to dinner, Aunt Norris cannot resist a jibe, by warning the latter about 'the nonsense and folly of peoples stepping out of their rank and trying to appear above themselves'. When Aunt Norris goes on to suggest that Fanny could walk to the dinner engagement, Sir Thomas overrules her in no uncertain manner and orders the carriage to call and collect her.

At the parsonage Henry Crawford, echoing the views of his sister Mary, declares that the most interesting topic in the world was 'how to make money – how to turn a good income into a better'. He subsequently declares his intention to 'make Fanny Price [fall] in love with me'. At this, Mary tells him that it is her wish that he does not make Fanny unhappy, 'for she is as good a little creature as ever lived and has a great deal of feeling'.

When Fanny's brother William, who is in the Royal Navy, visits Mansfield Park, Fanny declares that she has

> never known so much felicity in her life ... Children of the same family, the same blood, with the same first associations

and habits, have some means of enjoyment in their power, which no subsequent connections can supply . . .

William presents Fanny with an amber cross, whereupon Mary Crawford invites her to choose a necklace to wear with it. Mary does not tell Fanny that the necklace she chooses had been previously purchased by her brother Henry who has designs on her. In other words, Fanny has been tricked. When Edmund also presents Fanny with a chain for William's cross, she says she will return the one given to her by Mary. However, he persuades her not to do so. At a ball held by Sir Thomas at Mansfield Park, Fanny resolves the dilemma in which she finds herself by wearing both Edmund's chain and Mary's necklace with her cross.

When Sir Thomas asks Fanny to lead the way and open the ball, she is overcome:

She could hardly believe it. To be placed above so many elegant young women! The distinction was too great.

Sir Thomas, for his part, acknowledges that whereas his family had been kind to Fanny, she was now 'quite as necessary to us'.

Edmund is dismayed when Mary tells him that this will be the last time she will ever dance with him. 'She never has danced with a clergyman, she says, and she never will,' he tells Fanny. Not only that, but Mary confirms her lack of feelings for Edmund by telling Fanny that she regards him as no more than a 'friendly acquaintance'.

Henry Crawford informs his sister Mary that he is determined to marry Fanny Price. He tells Fanny that his uncle the Admiral has promoted her brother William to be a lieutenant in the Navy and confirms that it was he (Henry) who was instrumental in persuading him to do so. Moreover, 'Every thing he had done for William was to be placed at the account of his excessive and unequalled attachment to her'. Fanny is horrified. 'But you are not thinking of me. I know it is all nothing,' she says. Mary compounds the situation by assuming that Fanny has decided to marry her brother and offering her congratulations.

Shortly afterwards Sir Thomas tells Fanny that Henry Crawford has arrived to see her. Fanny responds by telling Sir Thomas that she intends to refuse Henry's offer of marriage on the grounds that she is 'so perfectly convinced' that she could never make him happy and that she should be miserable herself. Aunt Norris then weighs in by criticising Fanny for her independent and secretive spirit. Sir Thomas, having tried his utmost in the matter, finally relents, saying that he will not attempt to persuade Fanny to marry against her will. 'Your happiness and advantage are all that I have in view.' As for Lady Bertram, she tries to cheer Fanny up by saying: 'The next time Pug [her dog] has a litter, you shall have a puppy.'

Nevertheless, Fanny finds herself besieged on all sides. Henry Crawford turns on the charm to persuade her:

My conduct shall speak for me – absence, distance, time shall speak for me. – They, shall prove, that as far as you can be deserved by any body, I do deserve you.

When Fanny tells Edmund that she and Henry are 'totally unalike . . . We have not one taste in common. We should be miserable', he says he believes her to be mistaken. Mary openly admits to Fanny that her brother Henry 'has now and then been a sad flirt and cared very little for the havock he might be making in young ladies' affections'; at which Fanny shakes her head and declares, 'I cannot think well of a man who sports with any woman's feelings'. When Mary says she believes Henry will love Fanny forever, 'Fanny could not avoid a faint smile . . .'

At Sir Thomas's suggestion, Fanny returns to her family in Portsmouth. The welcome, however, is not what she might have hoped for. Her father is pre-occupied with his son William and her mother has 'neither leisure nor affection to bestow on Fanny'. Henry Crawford arrives, saying that he cannot bear to be separated from her any longer, and she finds him 'much more gentle, obliging, and attentive to other peoples' feelings than he had ever been at Mansfield'. Fanny receives a letter from Edmund who is clearly still in love with Mary; she fears for him. 'He will marry her and be poor and miserable . . . She loves nobody but herself and her brother.'

Lady Bertram writes to Fanny to tell her that her son Tom has had a fall in London after 'a good deal of drinking' and has now developed a fever. Fanny also receives a letter from Mary Crawford to say that if Tom were to die, Edmund would become heir to Sir Thomas's estate, and it was Mary's opinion that 'wealth and consequence could fall into no hands more deserving of them'. The letter makes Fanny despise Mary even more in that she can, apparently, forgive Edmund for being a clergyman but only 'under certain conditions of wealth'.

Edmund writes to Fanny again saying that his sister Julia has eloped with their brother Tom's friend John Yates. It is also rumoured, and finally confirmed, that the Bertrams' elder daughter Maria has left her husband Mr Rushworth for Henry Crawford. In her judgement of Henry, Fanny is therefore completely vindicated. She is then summoned back to Mansfield Park, at Sir Thomas's behest, in order that she might comfort his wife Lady Bertram in all her family troubles.

Fanny learns from Edmund that Mary blames *her* for the debacle, in that had she accepted Henry's proposal of marriage he 'would have been too happy and too busy to want any other object', and 'would have taken no pains to be on terms with Mrs [Maria] Rushworth again'. Fanny calls this behaviour on Mary's part cruel. Edmund's eyes are now, at last, fully opened to Mary's character. 'How I have been deceived!' he says.

Jane Austen concludes *Mansfield Park* by saying that Fanny, in spite of everything, was a happy creature in that 'she had sources of delight that must force their way'. Not only that, but when she returned to Mansfield Park, 'she was useful, she was beloved; she was safe from Mr Crawford'. Also, Sir Thomas, even in his melancholy state of mind, was able to give her his 'perfect approbation and increased regard'. Most importantly of all, Edmund was 'no longer the dupe of Miss Crawford'. In fact, he admitted, 'even in the midst of his late infatuation', to Fanny's mental superiority. In other words, Fanny had been able to discern the truth about Mary Crawford, whereas he had not. Edmund and Fanny marry and, on Dr Grant's death, move into the parsonage at Mansfield Park.

So what is the message of *Mansfield Park*? It is the story of a young woman who starts life in a lower middle-class family in Portsmouth and becomes, to all intents and purposes, the mistress of Mansfield Park. How does she achieve this? By a steadfastness of character; by an unwillingness to condone or become involved in the schemes of others with which she disapproves, and by refusing an offer of matrimony from some-one who may be rich, but whom she knows can never make her happy. Even when she feels 'deserted by everybody' she does not abandon her principles. Her happiness is something which comes from within; it is not dependant on the wealth or patronage of others. Fortunately for Fanny, her strengths are recognised by Sir Thomas Bertram and latterly, by his younger son Edmund.

Fanny, a beacon of light in an often dark world, has many tribulations to bear: the spitefulness of Aunt Norris; the indifference of her parents when she returns to Portsmouth; the duplicity of Henry and Mary Crawford and the naivety of the love-struck Edmund. Nevertheless, she behaves unselfishly even when all hope of a union between herself and Edmund appears to have vanished: always making his happiness her primary consideration.

Also, although Fanny's parents have little time for her, there are strong indications in the novel of the importance Fanny places on her loving relationship with her brother William, and latterly with her sister Susan; such relationships being regarded by her as uniquely to be treasured.

In January 1813, a few days before the publication of her novel *Pride and Prejudice*, Jane's sister Cassandra left Chawton to visit Steventon, a journey of 14 miles. She was therefore absent when the author's copy of the novel arrived from the publishers, and all Jane could do was write to her: 'I want to tell you that I have got my own darling child [i.e. the novel] from London'.[1]

Jane's letters indicate that her mother's health was particularly bad during that year. For example, in the February:

> My Mother slept through a good deal of Sunday . . . & even yesterday she was but poorly. She is pretty well again today, & I am in hopes may not be much longer a Prisoner [i.e. in the house].[2]

Jane's cousin Eliza, Henry's wife, had also been ill for almost a year, and she was now fading fast. Henry sent for Jane to come to London, to Sloane Street where they now lived, to comfort her. She died on 25 April 1813, aged 50.

In June 1813, Charles's two eldest daughters Cassandra and Harriet came to stay with their Aunts Jane and Cassandra in Hampshire. From mid-September to November of that year, it was Jane's turn to stay at Godmersham Park.

Jane sent her brother Francis a long letter in early July. In it, she said that the previous January she had learnt, from the newspaper, that the Revd Samuel Blackall had married Susannah, 'eldest daughter of James Lewis Esq. of Clifton, late of Jamaica'.[3] The previous year Blackall had achieved his wish of becoming Rector of North Cadbury, Somerset and could therefore now afford a wife.

Jane had previously described Blackall as 'a peice of Perfection' and someone whom she would 'always recollect with regard'. Now, in respect of his new wife, she stated as follows:

> I would wish Miss Lewis to be of a silent turn & rather igno-rant, but naturally intelligent & wishing to learn; fond of cold veal pies, green tea in the afternoon, & a green window-blind at night.[4]

This smacks of sour grapes on Jane's part. She knew that Blackall was a lively and intelligent man, so if she had had his best interests at heart, she would naturally have wished for his partner to be of a similar nature. Instead, she expresses the hope that Susannah Lewis will prove to be dull and staid. In other words, Jane hopes that Blackall will be punished for not choosing her instead; she who had all the requisite qualities.

So why had he not married Jane? After all, she was still a single woman and in good health. Was it, as has already been suggested, because of intervention by Cassandra?

Despite receiving this piece of portentous news about Blackall, Jane still found it possible to think of her brother. She wrote to Francis:

My Dearest Frank . . .

God bless you. – I hope you continue beautiful & brush your hair, but not all off. – We join in an infinity of love.

Yrs very affectly,
Jane Austen.[5]

At about this time, Jane's niece Frances ('Fanny') Knight observed that her Aunt Jane 'suffered sadly with her face'.[6] Years later, Fanny's sister Elizabeth ('Lizzy') recalled seeing Jane walk

with head a little to one side, and sometimes a very small cushion pressed against her cheek, if she were suffering from face-ache, as she not infrequently did in later life.[7]

What the Knight sisters were observing in Jane were attacks of trigeminal neuralgia, caused by a dysfunction of the trigeminal (or 5th cranial) nerve which supplies the face. The pain is severe and comes in paroxysms, and the disorder is believed to be due to compression of the nerve in the bony canal between the brain and the face, in which it lies.

Jane told Cassandra that their mother had improved and was 'no more in need of Leeches'. (A leech is a large aquatic blood-sucking worm used by the medical profession for the purpose of blood-letting, which was considered to be beneficial.) Nevertheless, James E. Austen-Leigh declares that during the last years of her life, Mrs Austen 'endured continual pain, not only patiently but with characteristic cheerfulness'. (In fact, she lived on until 1827).[8]

In September 1813 Jane sent Francis an even longer letter, packed with news and addressed to: 'Captain Austen, HMS *Elephant*, Baltic.'[9]

The following month gave Jane the opportunity of seeing her youngest brother, Charles, when he and his wife Frances arrived at Godmersham Park, where she was staying. She said warmly:

> Here they are, safe and well, just like their own nice selves, Fanny (Frances) looking as neat & white this morning as possible, and dear Charles all affectionate, placid, quiet, chearful good humour.[10]

In a letter to her niece Anna Austen, written in mid-September 1814, Jane gave a clue as to how she obtained ideas for the characters of her novels when she said, '3 or 4 Families in a Country Village is the very thing to work on'.[11]

❧ 17 ❧

Jane and Eliza: Two Opposites

Jane had many reasons to be grateful to her cousin Eliza: for encouraging her in her music, her singing, her manners and deportment, and not least, her writing. However, there were aspects of Eliza's character with which Jane would have neither empathised, nor approved.

For example, when Eliza enlightened her about the goings on at the French Court – and at the English Court also – Jane may not have been particularly impressed. This was because her heart was firmly rooted at Steventon, in the depths of her beloved Hampshire countryside, and amidst those familiar faces with which she came into contact on a day-to-day basis, as one of her poems indicates:

Happy the Lab'rer in his Sunday Cloathes! –
In light-drab coat, smart waistcoat, well-darn'd Hose
And hat upon his head to Church he goes;
As oft with conscious pride he downward throws
A glance upon the ample Cabbage rose
Which stuck in Buttonhole regales his nose,
He envies not the gayest London Beaux.
In Church he takes his seat among the rows,
Pays to the Place the reverence he owes,
Likes best the Prayers whose meaning least he knows,
Lists to the Sermon in a softening Doze,
And rouses joyous at the welcome close.

Eliza wrote many letters to her cousin Phylly Walter, and although Jane was clearly not privy to the content of these letters, they provide a useful guide as to her character, opinions and beliefs. They indicate that Eliza may not always have behaved in a manner which Jane, as the daughter of a clergyman and a devout Christian herself, would have condoned. For instance, when Eliza tells Phylly that she has been invited to the Coronation Ball (held to commemorate the coronation of King George III, which had taken place on 22 September 1761), she (Eliza)

> hesitated for some time, but at length consented, because I always find that the most effectual mode of getting rid of a temptation is to give way to it.[1]

Amusing as this comment may be, there may have been more than a grain of truth in it, and not just in regard to coronation balls.

Eliza tells Phylly that she hopes to have

> a full & particular account of all your Flirtations. Is there not a certain Clergyman some where in your neighbourhood that You contrive to flirt with a little? Adieu My aimiable Friend think of me & think of me with some affection since, not with-standing all my faults I love you most sincerely.[2]

This begs the question, was Eliza herself a flirt? An (unnamed) daughter of Anna Lefroy supports the notion that yes, she was, when she states:

> I believe the *ci-devant* Countess [French nobility of the *ancien régime*], who was an extremely pretty woman, was a great flirt, and during her brief widowhood flirted with all her Steventon cousins, our Grandfather [James Austen] inclusive.[3]

On the other hand, the whole tenor of Jane's novels indicates that she herself would hardly have approved of flirting, and least of all with a gentleman of the cloth. Eliza, however, did have certain scruples. She said:

I have made one conquest, who has between thirty & forty thousand pr. [per] Annum, but unfortunately he also has a Wife, so that I cannot even indulge myself in a little flirtation.[4]

She makes another comment to Phylly that Jane would undoubtedly have considered vulgar and in poor taste had she heard it:

I do not hear that Mrs. James Austen [Jane's sister in law] is breeding, but I conclude it is so, for a Parson cannot fail of having a numerous Progeny.[5]

In marrying the Comte de Feuillide it is evident that Eliza's main concerns were for money and status. With the Comte, she said she was

... mistress of an easy fortune with the prospect of a very ample one, add to these the advantages of rank & title & the numerous & brilliant acquaintance, amongst whom I can flatter myself I have some sincere friends, & you will unite with me in saying I have reason to be thankful to Providence for the lot fallen to my share ...[6]

When it came to assessing Henry as a prospective second husband, Eliza used the same criteria. She commented to Phylly:

I suppose you know that our Cousin Henry is now Captain, Pay Master & Adjutant. He is a very lucky young Man and bids fair to possess a considerable Share of Riches & Honour; I believe he has now given up all thoughts of the church, and he is right for he is certainly not so fit for a parson as a soldier.[7]

Clearly, Eliza could not imagine anyone wishing to marry a clergyman who depended solely on his income, as this comment to Phylly indicates:

I heard the confirmation of our old friend Dr Thomas Woodman's having taking orders which surprises everyone, as his Father can give him a very handsome fortune.[8]

Did Eliza marry the Comte for love, also? Hardly, for as Phylly confirms:

The Countess has many amiable qualities . . . [however] for her husband she professes a large share of respect, esteem and the highest opinion of his merits, but confesses that Love is not of the number on her side.[9]

In fact, Eliza could not even envisage falling in love. Do not imagine, she tells Phylly, referring to Germany, Flanders and France, which she had previously visited,

that I have left my Heart in either of those places . . . to tell you the Truth I don't think either You or I very likely to lose either our gaiety or peace of mind for any male creature breathing.[10]

As for the marriage ceremony itself, Eliza declared: 'I never was but at one wedding in my life and that appeared a very stupid Business to me'.[11]

Did Eliza marry *Henry* for love? Indeed, there is no mention of the word in the following statement to Phylly, in which she appears to view Jane's brother with a scarcely veiled contempt. Eliza described

> the pleasure of having my own way in every thing, for Henry well knows that I have not been accustomed to controul and should probably behave rather awkwardly under it, and therefore like a wise Man he has no will but mine, which to be sure some people would call spoiling me, but [I] know is the best way of managing me.[12]

In other words, everything must be on her terms. To Jane, of course, for someone to marry a person with whom they were not in love would have been absolutely anathema.

Phylly stated that, despite everything, Eliza's religion [i.e. the Christian faith] 'is not changed'.[13] However, the latter evidently paid the price for her 'dissipated life' for, as she remarked regretfully:

> Poor Eliza must be left at last friendless & alone. The gay and dissipated life she has long had so plentiful a share of has not insur'd her friends among the worthy; on the contrary many who otherwise have regarded her have blamed her conduct & will resign her acquaintance. I always felt concerned and pitied her thoughtlessness.[14]

Leaving aside their common interest in music and poetry, it is difficult to imagine two people whose views were so deeply contrasting than Jane and Eliza, and not surprisingly, Jane could not resist making her cousin a character – albeit thinly disguised – in one of her novels: that novel being *Mansfield Park*.

༖ 18 ༖

'Mary Crawford':
The Reincarnation of Eliza

A clue that Jane may have had Eliza in mind when she was writing her novel *Mansfield Park*, is given by the fact that the fictitious Lady Bertram possesses a dog by the name of 'Pug', whom she dotes on and spoils unutterably. Eliza also possessed a pug (this being the generic name for a breed of toy dog) and treated the creature with the same indulgence. She came by it in the following way. On 7 November 1796 Eliza reminded her cousin Philadelphia Walter ('Phylly') that she had promised to acquire a dog for her. Eliza says, 'I live in hope of dear Pug's arrival. Pray get him for me if possible'. By the following month it is clear that Phylly has obliged, because Eliza states that she is now in possession of her Pug and 'shall joyfully receive as many more as you can provide for me'. Not only that, but Eliza has consulted her doctor about the dog and the administration of 'Vapour Baths, which he has prescribed for him'.[1] Eliza did, in fact, go on to possess several pug dogs. However, it was not Lady Bertram who Jane had in mind for Eliza, but another of the principal characters in the story: Mary Crawford.

What similarities are there between the real life Eliza and the fictional Mary? Eliza, from her portrait, is an attractive woman with long, wavy, auburn hair and large brown eyes reminiscent of a painting by Rubens, but not, perhaps, a classical beauty; Mary is 'remarkably pretty'. Eliza is comfortably placed, thanks to the generosity of Warren Hastings; Mary is 'possessed of

£20,000'. Both have good connections: Eliza is accustomed to mixing in the upper echelons of society at both the French and the English Courts; Mary's brother Henry has 'a good estate in Norfolk'. Both ladies are fond of London (and in Eliza's case, Paris also); both play the harp and the pianoforte and love to sing; both participate in amateur theatricals. Moreover, both are strong-minded characters used to having their own way.

Both Mary and Eliza are essentially townspeople who are not altogether comfortable in the countryside. For example, when Mary complains that she cannot find a wagon or cart for hire in the village on which to transport her harp, Edward feels obliged to point out that yes, indeed, this would be difficult in the middle of harvest time. How different this is from London, says Mary, where 'every thing is to be got with money'. As for Eliza, she was accustomed to the French Court and later to the English Court, and yet her letters to Phylly indicate that in later years she had become more attuned to country living.

Just as Eliza has lived in France and speaks the language fluently, so too in Mansfield Park does Mary show that she has a knowledge of that country and its people. Mary says, in reference to the vanity of a former French King:

> To say the truth, I am something like the famous Doge [Chief of State] at the court of Lewis [Louis] XIV; and may declare that I see no wonder in the shrubbery equal to seeing myself in it.

And Mary tells her sister Mrs Grant:

> If you can persuade Henry [her brother] to marry, you must have the address of a Frenchwoman. All that English abilities can do has been tried already.

(Is this Jane telling us in code that Eliza had tried, without success, to find a suitable English husband before she married the Count?) Apart from these superficial similarities, there is evidence that Mary was like Eliza in more fundamental ways.

Mary declares that, 'A large income, is the best recipe for happiness I ever heard of'. And Fanny Price says of Mary, 'She had only learnt to think nothing of consequence but money'. The obvious way to achieve wealth was, of course, to marry and this was exactly what Mary had in mind. 'Matrimony was her object, provided she could marry well'. Her advice was that 'every body should marry as soon as they can do it to advantage'. However, Mary warns that for those like herself, who marry for money, there are pitfalls. She says:

> [marriage] is, of all transactions, one in which people expect the most from others, and are least honest themselves . . . It is a manoeuvring business. I know so many who have married in the full expectation and confidence of some one particular advantage in the connection, or accomplishment of good quality in the person, who have found themselves entirely deceived, and been obliged to put up with exactly the reverse!

Is this Jane telling us that Eliza (Mary) was disappointed in her marriage to the Comte? After all, Jean-François Capot was not a genuine count. He was

> [the] son of a provincial lawyer who had risen to become mayor of Nérac, a town in the province of Guinne, in the south-west of France, where the family owned a small estate.

For Mary, there are certain classes of people who it would be folly to marry. For example, she is dismissive of Edmund's intention to become a clergyman and declares, 'A clergyman is nothing', by which she meant that a man of the cloth, by virtue of his position in life, cannot aspire to wealth. When Mary declares to Edmund her intention to become very rich, he in turn declares that his intentions are only 'not to be poor'. To this, Mary replies:

> Be honest and poor by all means – but I shall not envy you; I do not much think I shall even respect you. I have a much greater respect for those that are honest and rich.

Mary also demonstrates her disdain for the clergy by expressing the opinion that, in former times, 'parsons were very inferior even to what they are now'.

According to Mary, Edmund's salvation would be if his brother Tom were to die, thereby leaving him to inherit Mansfield Park. Edmund would then be a much more attractive proposition as a husband. At this, the horrified Fanny remarks dryly, 'Edmund would be forgiven for being a clergyman, it seemed, under certain conditions of wealth'.

Was Mary Crawford a flirt, as Eliza was alleged to be? No, because for Jane this would have been a step too far, as she would have risked offending both Eliza, who would certainly have recognised herself in the novel, and her husband Henry. Instead, she makes Mary's brother Henry the flirt. As previously quoted, Mary says:

> He [Henry] is the most horrible flirt that can be imagined. If your Miss Bertrams do not like to have their hearts broke, let them avoid Henry.

So who is there, in Mansfield Park, to counteract the influence of Mary? Why, Fanny Price, of course, who in turn is undoubtedly a vehicle for Jane's own thoughts and feelings.

When Mary played the harp to Fanny (as Eliza undoubtedly did to Jane), the latter is described as being 'so full of wonder at the performance'.

In a similar way, Jane's youngest brother Charles is represented by Fanny's older brother William, who is a sailor in the Royal Navy and who makes his sister the present of an amber cross.

Referring to Mary, Fanny says, 'She might love, but she did not deserve Edmund by any other sentiment'. Fanny believed there was scarcely a second feeling in common between them [which she follows up with the words]: 'She loves nobody but herself and her brother'.

In *Mansfield Park* Jane mirrors the Stevenson amateur theatrical performances which Eliza enjoyed so much. When the Honourable John Yates, a friend of Tom Bertram, arrives on the scene and suggests that they 'raise a little theatre' – i.e. put on a play, Edmund has reservations, believing that were they to do so, this would 'show great want of feeling on my father's account, absent as he is'. Edmund also believes that the particular play they have chosen, *Lovers' Vows*, is 'exceedingly unfit for private representation'. (This was a real life play by the German August von Kotzebue, written in 1780 and entitled *Das Kind der Liebe* – 'Child of Love', and adapted by actress, novelist and dramatist Elizabeth Inchbald. As the title suggests, it featured seduction and an illegitimate birth.)

In *Mansfield Park*, although it is not Mary who chooses the play which is to be performed, when the choice is made she condones it, and eagerly expresses the wish to participate in it. Perhaps the real life Eliza did actually choose some of the plays which were performed at Steventon – notably the more risque ones, and perhaps this offended Jane and one or more of her brothers. It may even have come to the notice of the Revd Austen who, like his fictitious counterpart Sir Tomas

Bertram, would have considered such plays to be inappropriate and unseemly.

Jane, typically, could not portray Mary as being all bad, and when the latter comforts Fanny, after her Aunt Norris pressurises her [unsuccessfully] to accept the hand of Mary's brother Henry, Jane writes: 'Fanny did not love Miss Crawford; but she felt very much obliged to her for her present kindness'. Perhaps this was how Jane viewed Eliza, who had shown her acts of kindness but whom she could not bring herself to love.

Due to the prolonged periods which Eliza spent with the Austens at Steventon, it is likely that Jane was familiar with her views on the subjects discussed above. However, it is unlikely that she challenged her cousin on these views. After all, there was a disparity in their ages, Eliza being more than a decade her senior, and in their position, Eliza had rubbed shoulders with royalty and aristocracy, both English and French. Nevertheless, to hear Eliza being disparaging about the clergy, cynical about marriage and concerned with personal gain rather than with true love, must have caused Jane a certain amount of anguish.

Instead, Jane, as Fanny Price, made Eliza, as Mary Crawford, her protagonist in *Mansfield Park*, and in doing so she was not only able to give vent to her emotions, but also to create that tension between two opposites which is essential for the success of any novel. How paradoxical, therefore, that Eliza, with whom Jane had little or nothing in common in a spiritual or moral sense, became pivotal to the narrative of *Mansfield Park*.

Eliza was left 'friendless and alone'. On the other hand Mary, who had suffered 'disappointment in the course of the last half year' (largely because of the irresponsible behaviour of her brother), had the good fortune to be taken in by her half-sister Mrs Grant. As for Henry, his punishment was to suffer 'wretchedness' and 'vexation' for tampering with Fanny's feelings, and thereby destroying any chance which he may have had of winning her heart.

As already mentioned, Eliza died in April 1813 and *Mansfield Park* was published the following year. The timing of the publication was probably not a coincidence in that Jane, for obvious reasons, would probably not have wished the novel to be published while Eliza was still alive.

Eliza had married, only to become a widow when her husband the Comte was executed. She had finally married Jane's brother Henry. When Eliza died, Jane was aged only 37. Would Jane herself find a partner, albeit belatedly? If so, unlike her cousin, she would surely marry for love.

🌸 19 🌸

Emma

Emma was written between 21 January 1814 and 29 March 1815, and published in 1816 by John Murray. The heroine, Emma Woodhouse, is described as 'handsome, clever, and rich, with a comfortable home and happy disposition'. However, she is lacking in the ability to judge character, which will become apparent in due course. Emma lives at Hartfield with her father, who is described as 'most affectionate' and 'indulgent'. She has an elder sister Isabella, who is married to Mr John Knightley, the brother of the hero of the story, Mr Knightley of Donwell Abbey. Isabella lives in London.

Mr Knightley is described as 'a sensible man about seven or eight – and – thirty' who was 'a very old [longstanding] and intimate friend of the family'. He was also 'one of the few people who could see faults in Emma Woodhouse, and the only one who ever told her of them'.

Miss Taylor, Emma and Isabella's governess for a period of sixteen years, has recently left the household to be married to Mr Weston of nearby Randalls. Mr Weston's first wife was Miss Churchill, 'of a great Yorkshire family'. The couple had a son Frank, but three years after the marriage his mother died whereupon the boy was adopted by his uncle and aunt, the Churchills; since then he has not visited his father. At the age of 21, Frank adopted the surname of Churchill, rather than Weston.

When Emma boasts to Knightley that it was she who brought Mr Weston and Miss Taylor together, he denies it, saying that this was simply due to 'a lucky guess' on Emma's part. When Emma suggests that she now intends to look for a wife for Mr Elton, the vicar of Highbury, Knightley's advice to her is, 'Invite him to dinner, Emma, and help him to the best of the fish and the chicken, but leave him to chuse his own wife'.

In the evenings, Emma's father Mr Woodhouse enjoys play-ing cards with the Westons, Mr Knightley, Mr Elton, Mrs Bates (the widow of the former vicar of Highbury) and her daughter Miss Bates, and Mrs Goddard (mistress of a boarding school). To one of these social gatherings Mrs Goddard asks if she can bring Miss Harriet Smith, a 17-year-old who is a pupil at her school. Harriet is described as being 'not clever', but with 'a sweet, docile, grateful disposition; was totally free from conceit; and only desiring to be guided by any one she looked up to'.

Emma finds Harriet pleasing both in her manners and in her person, and is 'quite determined to continue the acquaintance'. But she disapproves of the farming family, the Martins, with whom Harriet has been associating and whom she assumes 'must be coarse and unpolished. The yeomanry are precisely the order of people with whom I feel I can have nothing to do.' Instead, Emma is determined to introduce Harriet 'into good society', where she 'would form her opinions and her manners'. She says to Harriet:

> The misfortune of your birth ought to make you particularly careful as to your associates. There can be no doubt of your being a gentleman's daughter, and you must support your claim to that station by every thing within your power. [Harriet is, in fact, the daughter of a London tradesman.]

Furthermore, it is Emma's view that, while farmer Robert Martin is 'remarkably plain' and 'very clownish', Mr Elton, in comparison, is 'good humoured, cheerful, obliging, and gentle'. The latter becomes, therefore, 'the very person fixed on by Emma for driving the young farmer out of Harriet's head'.

With regard to the intimacy between Emma and Harriet, Mr Knightley has serious reservations. In fact, he believes that Harriet is:

> the very worst sort of companion that Emma could possibly have. She knows nothing herself, and looks upon Emma as knowing every thing. She is a flatterer in all her ways . . .

Emma proceeds to use every means within her power to bring Harriet and Mr Elton together. When she makes a sketch of Harriet, and Mr Elton volunteers to take it to London to have it framed, Emma hopes this will endear the clergyman to the subject of her portrait. There is a stumbling block to Emma's plans, however, when Harriet receives a letter from Robert Martin containing 'a direct proposal of marriage'. Emma puts doubts in Harriet's mind about the suitability of Robert, and tells her that if she has any reservations, 'she certainly ought to refuse him'. Finally, she smiles sweetly and says: 'Not for the world, would I advise you either way. You must be the best judge of your own happiness.'

On the strength of this advice, Harriet decides to refuse Robert. Knightley takes the opposite view and describes Robert as an excellent young man. In fact, when the latter comes to ask his advice, Knightley has no hesitation in advising him to marry. Therefore, when Knightley hears that Emma has persuaded Harriet to refuse Robert, he is appalled. Despite this, Emma maintains that, even though

> Mr Martin may be the richest of the two . . . he is undoubtedly her [Harriet's] inferior as to rank in society – the sphere in which she moves is much above his – It would be a degradation.

Knightley guesses that Emma has decided on Elton as being a suitable partner for Harriet, but thinks that her efforts in this direction 'will be all labour in vain'. He says, 'Elton may talk sentimentally, but he will act rationally . . . I am convinced that he does not mean to throw himself away'. Emma becomes more and more convinced of Mr Elton's interest in Harriet, not realising that it is she, Emma, who is the subject of his affection. Emma demonstrates that she is not totally devoid of feeling when she asks Knightley to reassure her that Robert 'is not very bitterly disappointed' at Harriet's refusal of him; Knightley disappoints her by replying, 'A man cannot be more so'.

Emma pursues her own ambitions by turning her attentions to Mr Frank Churchill. 'If she [Emma] were to marry, [then] he was the very person to suit her in age, character and condition'. But she is disconcerted when, on a return journey from a dinner party with the Westons at Randalls, Mr Elton seizes her hand, makes a declaration of his hopes, fears and adoration, and states that he is ready to die if she refuses him. With regard to Harriet as a potential partner Elton says scornfully: 'I never thought of Miss Smith in the whole course of my existence'.

Knightley expresses his disapproval of Frank Churchill, whom he considers to be negligent in that he has failed to visit his father. He feels sure that if Frank wished to see his father, then 'he would have contrived it'. When Emma makes excuses for Frank, Knightley remains unmoved. 'There is one thing, Emma, which a man can always do, if he chuses and that is, his duty'.

Emma and Harriet visit Mrs and Miss Bates, where Emma is told, by the latter, that her [Miss Bates'] niece Jane Fairfax, is shortly to come and stay with her. Jane is an orphan, whose adoptive parents, the Campbells, are soon to make a visit to Ireland. When Emma is duly introduced to Jane she finds her very reserved. Meanwhile, Mr Elton marries the wealthy Augusta Hawkins of Bath.

Frank finally arrives at Randalls to visit his father Mr Weston. Emma is introduced to Frank and forms a good opinion of him. However, this opinion is 'a little shaken' when she hears 'that he was gone off to London, merely to have his hair cut'. Mr Knightley considers Frank to be a 'trifling, silly fellow'. When Frank returns home to Yorkshire, Emma persuades herself that he has fallen in love with her.

As time goes by, Emma values Harriet's affection more and more. 'There is no charm equal to tenderness of heart', she says. 'There is nothing to be compared to it'. And she confesses that, although her 'dear father' possesses it, and her sister Isabella, and Harriet all possess it, she herself does not, even though she knows 'how to prize and respect it'.

Emma suspects that Mr Knightley may be in love with Jane Fairfax. He denies it saying that although Jane is a very charming young woman, 'she has not the open temper which a man could wish for in a wife'. In other words, he finds Jane too reserved.

A ball is held at The Crown Inn at which Harriet, who has no partner, is snubbed by Mr Elton. When Knightley comes to her rescue by asking her to dance, Emma is gratified, and even more so when he declares that Harriet 'has some first-rate qualities which Mrs Elton is totally without'.

When Harriet goes for a walk and finds herself surrounded and threatened by some gypsy children, it is Frank Churchill who comes to her rescue. On an outing to Box Hill, Frank declares that he is too hot. Emma, who interprets this as a feebleness of character, says to herself, scornfully:

> I am glad I have done being in love with him. I should not like a man who is so soon discomposed by a hot morning.

Nonetheless, Frank indulges in a little flirting with Emma, who in turn insults Miss Bates, implying that her conversation is limited to saying only 'dull things'. At this, Knightley is not amused:

> How could you be so unfeeling to Miss Bates? How could you be so insolent in your wit to a woman of her character, age, and situation? She is poor; she has sunk from the comfort she was born to; and, if she lives to old age, must probably sink more. Her situation should secure your compassion, it was badly done indeed!

At this, Emma is filled with remorse. She resolves to pay a visit to Miss Bates in order to apologise for her behaviour.

When Frank asks Emma if she will choose a wife for him, it is Harriet who immediately springs to Emma's mind as being a suitable partner. And when Frank's aunt Mrs Churchill dies, Emma believes that this has removed an impediment to Frank and Harriet becoming attached to one another. However, Emma is horror-struck when Mrs Weston tells her that Frank has announced that he is already engaged to Jane Fairfax, and has been for some time. Emma is now concerned for Harriet, whom she had tacitly encouraged to love Frank. But she need not have worried, for Harriet declares that she does not care for Frank at all. 'Dear Miss Woodhouse, how could you so mistake me?' she asks, and then confesses that she is in love with someone who is 'infinitely superior'. Emma, to her consternation, deduces that she is speaking of Knightley:

> Mr Knightley and Harriet Smith! – such an elevation on her side! Such a debasement on his!

Knightley is under the impression that Emma is attached to Frank, but she denies it. However, she does admit that she was 'tempted by his attentions' and allowed herself 'to appear pleased. He has imposed on me but he has not injured me,' she says. Knightley then proposes to Emma, and she accepts him.

Frank then writes a long letter to Mrs Weston, explaining that he was obliged to keep his engagement to Jane Fairfax secret because he knew that his aunt, Mrs Churchill, would disapprove of the marriage. Jane apologises to Emma, explaining the reason why her manner had been so cold and artificial. Knightley is magnanimous about Frank, believing that his character will improve and, acquire from Jane's 'the steadiness and delicacy of principle that it wants'. Emma forgives Frank, and wishes him joy when he finally marries Jane.

Knightley complains that Emma always calls him 'Mr Knightley'. At this, she promises to call him George, but only once, and that will be on their wedding day. All ends well for Harriet too, when, with Knightley's contrivance, she marries Robert Martin – her first love.

The lesson to be learned from Emma is obvious: Do not behave as Emma did and meddle in other peoples love affairs!

Whatever plans Jane and Tom Lefroy may have had for their future lives, these plans were thwarted, allegedly, by people meddling in their affairs. Inter-marriage did take place between the Lefroys and the Austens when, on 8 November 1814, Benjamin (later the Revd) Lefroy, the late Mrs Lefroy's youngest son, married Anna, eldest daughter of the Revd James Austen, at Steventon Church. To Jane, this event must have seemed to be something of an irony.

On 18–20 November 1814, Jane found herself counselling her niece Fanny Knight, who consulted her about an affair of the heart. In advising Fanny, Jane revealed the qualities which she herself regarded as prerequisite in a husband, while at the same time pointing out to Fanny how rare it was to encounter the ideal candidate. Jane said, referring to the gentleman in question, Mr John Plumptre:

His situation in life, family, friends, & above all his Character – his uncommonly amiable mind, strict principals, just notions, good habits – all that you know so well how to value, All that really is of the first importance – everything of this nature pleads his cause most strongly.

She went on to say:

There are such beings in the World perhaps, one in a Thousand, as the Creature You & I should think perfection, where Grace & Spirit are united to Worth, where the Manners are equal to the Heart & Understanding, but such a person may not come in your way. . .[1]

How poignant these words seem, bearing in mind Jane's own disappointments in her quest for a suitable partner.

✿ 20 ✿

Persuasion

The novel was begun in 1815 and completed in August 1816. Jane provisionally entitled it *The Elliots* but it was published as *Persuasion* by John Murray in December 1818, after Jane's death.

Persuasion is, undoubtedly, Jane Austen's most profound work and has much to say about the nature of love – as expressed by a man for a woman and vice versa. The heroine is Anne Elliot whose 'elegance of mind and sweetness of character . . . placed her high with any people of real understanding'. However, in the eyes of both her father and her sister, she is nobody. 'Her word had no weight; her convenience was always to give way; – she was only Anne'. As regards to her appearance, Anne's 'bloom had vanished early' and she is described as 'faded', thin', and 'haggard', to the extent that her father was doubtful whether anybody would consider her as a potential marital partner.

Anne is one of three daughters: Elizabeth being the eldest and Mary, who is married to Charles Musgrove and lives at nearby Uppercross, the youngest. Their father Sir Walter Elliot, a widower of Kellynch Hall in Somersetshire, is a person to whom vanity is 'the beginning and the end' of his character, both in regard to his person and to his situation. For this reason, the only book he ever bothers to read is *The Baronetage of England*, in which all the titled people of the country are listed.

Lady Russell lives in the nearby village of Kellynch. Described as 'a sensible, deserving woman' she had been the late Lady

Elliot's great friend, and after her ladyship's death, she became, for Anne in particular, a replacement mother. The heir to the Kellynch Estate is the Elliot sisters' estranged cousin William Elliot Esq., who has married 'a rich woman of inferior birth'.

For years, Sir Walter has lived beyond his means and he is now persuaded, both by his lawyer Mr Shepherd and by Lady Russell, that the only way open to him, if he is to discharge the claims of his creditors, is to quit Kellynch Hall – which will be let. The family, in consequence, move to Bath, a place which Anne dislikes. However, Lady Russell – who does like Bath – will join them there for a part of every winter.

The new tenant of Kellynch Hall is Admiral Croft (who fought at the Battle of Trafalgar) and his wife. The Crofts have local connections in that Mrs Croft has a brother, Mr Wentworth, who had once been curate of nearby Monkford. When Anne learns of the connection between the Crofts and Mr Wentworth, she is disturbed. This is because the latter is the brother of Captain Frederick Wentworth, a commander in the Royal Navy.

Described as 'a remarkably fine young man, with a great deal of intelligence, spirit and brilliancy', Captain Wentworth had come to Somersetshire in the summer of 1806 to stay for a while with his brother at Monkford. He and Anne had met at a time when he 'had nothing to do, and she had hardly any body to love. . .' They fell deeply in love and became engaged. However, Sir Walter had not looked favourably on the association of his daughter with a person who had 'no connexions' and no fortune. Lady Russell was of the same mind, believing that the engagement was 'indiscreet, improper and hardly capable of success'. The outcome was that the couple had parted and Captain Wentworth left the country.

Although Anne had been acquainted with Captain Wentworth for only a few months, her regret at parting

from him persisted and had, for her, 'clouded every enjoyment of youth'. As a result, 'an early loss of bloom and spirits
had been their lasting effect'. That was seven years ago and
in the intervening period, no one 'had ever come within the
Kellynch circle, who could bare a comparison with Frederick
Wentworth', even though, on one occasion, Anne had received
a proposal of marriage from Charles Musgrove, who subsequently married her younger sister Mary.

Whereas Anne does not blame Lady Russell in any way, for
guiding her away from Captain Wentworth, she feels certain
that had she maintained her attachment to him, she would
now be a happier woman in consequence. Meanwhile, she
learns that the Captain has gained promotion and become a
wealthy man.

After the Crofts take possession of Kellynch Hall and the
Elliot family relocate to Bath, it is decided that Anne will not,
at first, accompany them. Instead, she will stay for a while with
her sister Mary at Uppercross, as the latter, 'who was always
thinking a great deal of her own complaints', declares that she
cannot possibly do without her (Anne). Anne misses Kellynch
greatly:

> [her] beloved home made over to others; all the precious rooms
> and furniture, groves, and prospects beginning to own [accept]
> other eyes and other limbs!

When Anne and Captain Wentworth are reunited once again,
it is not at Uppercross but at the Great House, the home of
the Musgrove family. On this occasion, all that happens is that
their eyes meet, with a bow on the one side and a curtsy on the
other. When Captain Wentworth has departed, Mary tells Anne
that her sister-in-law Henrietta Musgrove of Uppercross, had
asked Captain Wentworth what he thought of her (Anne). The

Captain had replied that Anne was 'so altered he should not have known her again'. Despite her mortification at hearing these words, Anne acknowledges the fact that the years have 'destroyed her youth and bloom'. What makes her feel even more wretched is that she herself has

> used him [Captain Wentworth] ill; deserted and disappointed him; and worse, she had shewn a feebleness of character in doing so . . . She had given him up to oblige others. It had been the effect of over-persuasion. It had been weakness and timidity.

The result is that from then on, whenever the two meet, the only conversation is 'what the commonest civility required. Now they were as strangers; nay, worse than strangers'.

It appears to Anne that Captain Wentworth is attracted to Charles Musgrove's sisters Henrietta and Louisa, though she is not sure which one he prefers. In the end she decides that he is not in love with either of them. 'They were more in love with him; yet there it was not love. It was a little fever of admiration. . .'

Anne, her sister Mary, the Musgrove sisters, and Captain Wentworth and Charles Musgrove go for a long walk. They encounter Admiral Croft and his wife who have taken a drive in their gig. When the Crofts offer a lift 'to any lady who might be particularly tired', Captain Wentworth takes the initiative by assisting Anne into the carriage. She is thereby impressed by 'his perception of her fatigue' and also by his 'resolution to give her rest'. In fact, she regards this as:

> proof of his own warm and amiable heart, which she could not contemplate without emotions so compounded with pleasure and pain, that she knew not which prevailed.

Captain Wentworth receives a letter from his friend Captain Harville, who has settled for the winter with his family at Lyme (Regis) on the Dorsetshire coast. Harville had been wounded two years previously and his health has been poor ever since. When Wentworth visits Lyme and describes the 'fine country' round about, Anne, Mary, Charles and his sisters Henrietta and Louisa, decide that they too would like to visit that place.

At Lyme, where the party stays at an inn, Anne is able to comfort Captain Benwick, a friend of Captain Harville, who is residing with him. Benwick is in low spirits, having been engaged to Harville's sister Fanny, who had died the previous summer while he was at sea. Anne feels that Benwick's chances of happiness are, if anything, better than hers. She cannot believe that he has 'a more sorrowing heart' than she has. He is also younger than her and she feels sure that he will rally again 'and be happy with another'. She also feels that Benwick is reading too much poetry and 'ventured to recommend a larger amount of prose in his daily study'. While they are in Lyme, they encounter William Elliot, the heir to Kellynch Hall.

When Anne is finally reunited with her family in Bath she finds that 'they have no inclination to listen to her'. Their conversation 'must be all their own'. William Elliot pays the Elliots a visit and attempts to make amends for his former neglect of the family. Lady Russell's opinion of him is an extremely favourable one and she believes that Anne and William would make a happy couple. Not only that, but were Anne to become the future mistress of Kellynch this would be 'the highest possible gratification' to her ladyship. But Anne has reservations about William, being suspicious of his sudden desire for a reconciliation with the family. She also distrusts him because:

[he is] not open. There was never any burst of feeling, any warmth and indignation or delight at the evil or good of others.

This, Anne sees as 'a decided imperfection' in his character.

While in Bath, Anne takes the trouble to call on her former governess Miss Hamilton – now Mrs Smith – a widow who is in poor health and 'unable even to afford herself the comfort of a servant'. She does, however, have a Mrs Rooke to nurse her.

When the Crofts visit Bath, Admiral Croft informs Anne that Captain Wentworth is also on his way there. When, subsequently, they catch sight of one another in the street, Anne experiences a mixture of 'agitation, pain, pleasure, a something between delight and misery'. They exchange pleasantries until William Elliot arrives and walks off with Anne, arm in arm.

Anne and Captain Wentworth attend a concert in the Octagon Room. They discuss Louisa Musgrove and Captain Benwick, who have formed an attachment to one another – something of which Wentworth disapproves. 'He is a clever man, a reading man – and I confess that I do consider his attaching himself to her, with some surprise'. They reminisce about Lyme, which to Anne's mind was a place of real beauty. William Elliot comes and sits next to Anne and begins to flatter her, even alluding to the fact that if he dared, he would make her a proposal of marriage. Anne's thoughts, however, are for Captain Wentworth, who suddenly approaches her in the middle of the concert to wish her goodnight. 'Is not this song worth staying for?' asks Anne, who does not wish him to leave. 'No, there is nothing worth my staying for' he replies sombrely.

Anne calls, once again, on Mrs Smith who apprises her of the real character of William Elliot:

[He] is a man without heart or conscience; a designing, wary, cold-blooded being, who thinks only of himself; who, for his own interest or ease, would be guilty of any cruelty, or any treachery that could be perpetrated without risk of his general character. He has no feeling for others. Those whom he has been the chief cause of leading into ruin, he can neglect and desert without the smallest compunction. He is totally beyond the reach of any sentiment of justice or compassion. Oh! he is black at heart, hollow and black!

She knows this because William was formerly an intimate friend of her late husband. William, continued Mrs Smith, was anxious to make his fortune in a quicker manner than his profession as a lawyer would allow. He was, therefore, 'determined to make it by marriage'. As for the honour of his family, he held it 'as cheap as dirt'. Anne finally concludes that William is 'evidently a disingenuous, artificial, worldly man, who has never had any better principle to guide him than selfishness'. She had been right to be suspicious of him, for having previously despised the baronetcy, he had suddenly become determined to renew his acquaintance with the family, solely with the object of inheriting the title and becoming Sir William.

At the White Hart Inn – where the Musgroves are lodging – Anne encounters Captain Wentworth and Captain Harville. While Wentworth composes a letter, Anne and Captain Harville discuss Captain Benwick. Harville shows Anne a portrait of Benwick which had been painted at Fanny's (Benwick's late fiancée and Harville's sister's) request. Benwick now intends to give this portrait to Louisa Musgrove. 'Poor Fanny! She would not have forgotten him so soon!' says Harville. Anne and Harville then debate whether it is men or women who love the longest or the strongest. The debate ends with Anne saying that the only privilege she claimed for her own sex was 'that of loving longest, when existence or when hope is gone'.

Captain Wentworth hands the letter he has written to Anne, then leaves the room. It reads as follows:

Tell me not that I am too late, that such precious feelings are
gone forever. I offer myself to you again with a heart even
more your own, than when you almost broke it eight years and
a half ago. Dare not say that man forgets sooner than woman,
that his love has an earlier death. I have loved none but you.
Unjust I may have been, weak and resentful I have been, but
never inconstant.

Anne encounters Wentworth again in Union Street where the
couple:

exchanged again, those feelings and those promises which had
once before seemed to secure everything, but which had been
followed by so many, many years of division and estrange-
ment. There they returned again into the past, more exquisitely
happy, perhaps, in their re-union, than when it had been first
projected; more tender, more tried, more fixed in a knowledge
of each other's character, truth and attachment. . .

Anne then makes excuses to Captain Wentworth for the
behaviour of Lady Russell, who had erred in the advice she
gave to her all those years ago. Yet Lady Russell was, 'in the
place of a parent', and her (Anne's) conscience would have suffered had she ignored her ladyship's advice. Now, it was Anne's
opinion that:

There was nothing less for Lady Russell to do, than to admit
that she had been completely wrong, and to take up a new set
of pretty opinions and of hopes.

Anne and Captain Wentworth are finally married and their
marriage recorded in the '*Baronetage*' by her father Sir Walter
Elliot – in his own handwriting.

In *Persuasion*, as is so often the case with Jane's novels, there are echoes of her own life. For example, a family being obliged to vacate their home (which happened to the Austens on more than one occasion) and an interfering person (Mrs Lefroy) taking it upon herself to destroy the happiness of a young couple in love. The heroine Anne not only reproaches herself for being dictated to by Lady Russell but, most significantly, she attributes her premature loss of youth and bloom to the tragedy which her ladyship created. (This implies that Jane may have attributed the fact of her own fading looks to a failed relationship. The truth, however, was that before she had completed *Persuasion*, she had begun to develop the symptoms and signs of a chronic illness. This will be discussed shortly). Also, Jane's brother Francis's adventures are reflected by Jane in her character Admiral Croft who had taken part 'in the Trafalgar action' – although, as already mentioned, Francis had narrowly missed the Battle of Trafalgar.

In the debate about love, Anne Elliot is surely echoing Jane's own thoughts when she says that although her heart had previously been broken (in Jane's case by both Tom Lefroy and probably by Samuel Blackall), she still loved, even when all hope was gone. Unlike Jane, however, Anne Elliot achieves a happy ending to her story.

Jane's brothers were never far from her thoughts. For instance, she speaks of the many people 'whom Edward's charity has reached'. She also takes a lively interest in his activities, as in her mention of 'some very fine chestnuts [trees]' which he had selected for planting at Godmersham Park.

Her other brother Henry's physician, Dr Matthew Baillie, was also physician to the Prince Regent. Not only did Baillie inform Jane that the Prince was a great admirer of her novels, but a request was subsequently made to Jane that she dedicate her novel *Emma* to the Prince – which, of course, she did. It was published in December 1815.

In 1816 Henry's banking house of Austen, Maunde and Tilson collapsed, and on 15 March he was declared bankrupt. He then took holy orders, whereupon his brother Edward presented him with the gift of a curacy at Bentley, near Chawton. (Henry subsequently became Rector of Steventon).

Jane was by now aged 40 and still a single woman – as was her sister Cassandra. Meanwhile, of her six brothers, five had married (but not George), and four had children. And yet, there was no jealousy on Jane's part – only regret, that thus far she had been unfortunate enough not to find a partner. Instead, she rejoiced at the happiness of her married brothers, together with that of her nephews and nieces (with the possible exception of James and his family, whom she considered to be money-grabbing). She also had to bear the brunt of looking after her ageing mother – who suffered from chronic ill health – and did occasionally complain when she believed one or other of her siblings were not pulling their weight in family matters.

Jane Austen: A Loss of Youth and Bloom

By almost all accounts Jane Austen, in her prime, was an attractive and vivacious woman who took a pride in her appearance, loved children (provided, of course, that they were well behaved) and loved to dance. Jane's niece Caroline Austen, born in 1805 and daughter of her brother James, said this about her aunt:

> Hers was the first face that I can remember thinking pretty . . . Her face was rather round than long – she had a bright, but not a pink colour – a clear brown complexion and very good hazle eyes. She was not, I believe an absolute beauty, but before she left Steventon she was established as a very pretty girl, in the opinion of most of her neighbours . . . Her hair, a darkish brown, curls naturally – it was in short curls round her face. She always wore a cap . . .[1]

Caroline also said that Jane's 'charm to children was great sweetness of manner – she seemed to love you, and you loved her naturally in return'.

Kathryn Sutherland, editor of James E. Austen-Leigh's *A Memoir of Jane Austen*, describes a 'lightly executed pencil-and-watercolour portrait' of Jane, made by Cassandra and dated around 1810 as, 'the only authentic representation known to exist'.[2] In it, she is depicted unsmiling with chubby cheeks, brown curls, and wearing a bonnet. However, R.W. Chapman describes another portrait, which is also believed to be of Jane and also in water-colour. This time, she is depicted side on, in an outfit of blue and white, with overskirt, petticoat and bonnet with white ribbon. The portrait is signed and dated by Cassandra 'C.E.A. 1804'.[3]

In late October 1798 Jane wrote humorously to Cassandra:

next week shall begin my operations on my hat, on which You know my principal hopes of happiness depend.[4]

In late December she told Cassandra that she had attended a ball and had danced twenty dances

without any fatigue – I was glad to find myself capable of being able to dance so much & with so much satisfaction as I did ...[5]

On 2 June 1799, writing from Bath, Jane told Cassandra that she looked forward, with pleasure, to a grand gala to be held shortly in Sydney Gardens where there was to be a concert with illuminations and fireworks.[6] And in January 1801 she told Cassandra that she 'shall want two new coloured gowns for the summer'.[7]

Ten years later, in late April 1811, Jane wrote to Cassandra to say that she had been described by the Revd Dr Wyndham Knatchbull (son of Sir Edward Knatchbull by his second wife Frances), as 'a pleasing looking young woman'. She said, 'That must do; – one cannot pretend to anything better now – [I am] thankful to have it continued a few years longer!'[8] Alas, for Jane it would only be for a few years.

Jane told Cassandra, in March 1814, that she was still concerned about her attire:

I have been ruining myself in black sattined ribbon with proper pe[a]rl edge & now I am trying to draw it up into [a] kind of Roses instead of putting it in plain double plaits.[9]

Early in 1816 it was clear that all was not well with Jane Austen. In *A Biographical Notice of the Author*, published in 1818, her brother Henry stated that, 'The symptoms of a decay, deep and incurable, began to shew themselves . . .'[10] Jane's niece Caroline said, 'I believe Aunt Jane's health began to fail some time before we knew she was really ill'.[11]

On 8–9 September that year Jane wrote to Cassandra, who had recently paid her a visit, saying:

> Thank you, my Back has given me scarcely any pain for many days. – I have an idea that agitation does it as much harm as fatigue, & that I was ill at the time of your going, from the very circumstance of your going.[12]

Three months later, Jane refused an invitation to dinner. She said, 'I was forced to decline it, the walk is beyond my strength (though I am otherwise very well)'.[13]

On 24 January 1817 Jane wrote to her friend Alethea Bigg as follows:

> I have certainly gained strength through the Winter & am not far from being well; & I think I understand my own case now so much better than I did, as to be able by care to keep off any serious return of illness. I am more & more convinced that Bile is at the bottom of all I have suffered, which makes it easy to know how to treat myself.[14]

Bile is a bitter, greenish-brown alkaline fluid which is produced by the liver, stored in the gall bladder, and secreted into the gut. It contains waste products and also enzymes, which break down fat and aid digestion. A bilious attack, which Jane appears to have suffered from at least one of, indicates vomiting of such severity as to cause the contents, not only of the stomach but also of its exit passage the duodenum, to reflux up into the oesophagus and mouth.

Little information is available for the month of February 1817, apart from the fact that Jane had pain in one knee which she wrapped in flannel. However, a letter of hers dated 23/25 March, and written to her favourite niece Fanny Knight, contains important information:

> I certainly have not been very well for many weeks, & about a week ago I was very poorly, I have had a good deal of fever at times & indifferent nights, but am considerably better now & recovering my Looks a little, which have been bad enough, black & white & every wrong colour. I must not depend upon being ever blooming again. Sickness is a dangerous Indulgence at my time of Life.[15]

Jane was evidently distressed by her changing facial appearance, yet she resigned herself to it in her typically courageous way.

At the beginning of April 1817 Jane's niece Caroline went to stay for a few days at Wyards, a mile north of Chawton, which was the home of her half-sister Anna and Anna's husband Ben Lefroy. From here, she visited Jane and reported as follows:

> She was keeping to her room but she said she would see us, and we went up to her – She was in her dressing gown and was sitting quite like an invalide in an arm chair – but she got up, and kindly greeted us – and then pointing to the seats which had been arranged for us by the fire, she said, 'There's a chair for the married lady, and a little stool for you, Caroline.'
>
> I was struck by the alteration in herself – She was very pale – her voice was weak and low and there was about her, a general appearance of debility and suffering; but I have been told that she never had much actual pain. She was not equal to the exer-

tion of talking to us, and our visit to the sick room was a very short one – Aunt Cassandra soon taking us away . . .[16]

In a letter to her brother Charles of 6 April 1817, Jane tells of further problems with her health:

I have been really too unwell the last fortnight to write any-thing that was not absolutely necessary. I have been suffering from a Bilious attack, attended with a good deal of fever. – I was so ill on friday & thought myself so likely to be worse that I could not but press for Cassandra's return, with Frank . . .[17]

The attacks, or crises, were becoming more severe, making Jane feel apprehensive at her rapid deterioration. Jane wrote a despairing letter to her friend Anne Sharp; it contains several more important clues as to from what she was suffering:

in spite of my hopes & promises when I wrote to you I have since been very ill indeed. An attack of my sad complaint seized me within a few days afterwards – the most severe I ever had – & coming upon me after weeks of indisposition, it reduced me very low. . . . My head was always clear, & I had scarcely any pain; my chief sufferings were from feverish nights, weakness & Languor.

She told Anne that she had arranged to go to Winchester so as to be under the care of a well-known surgeon there, Mr. Lyford.[18] This was Giles King Lyford, Surgeon-in-Ordinary at the County Hospital. (It will be remembered that Giles's uncle, John Lyford, surgeon of Basingstoke, had previously attended Jane's mother Mrs Austen).

Shortly afterwards Jane wrote to her nephew James E. Austen-Leigh, and said that her appearance was still distressing to her:

> I will not boast of my handwriting; neither that, nor my face
> have yet recovered their proper beauty, but in other respects I
> am gaining strength very fast.

She also told James that she was eating her meals in a rational
way and was employing herself, though lying on the sofa most
of the day.[19]

James E. Austen-Leigh describes how, during what was to
be Jane's final illness, 'two of her brothers, who were clergymen [i.e. James and Henry], lived near enough to Winchester
to be in frequent attendance'.[20]

Nowhere are Jane's loving feelings towards Cassandra made
clearer than in a letter that she wrote in May 1817 to Frances,
daughter of James Tilson (who was a partner in her brother
Henry's former London bank), when she was seriously ill.
Whatever their past differences may have been, all was now
forgiven and forgotten. Jane wrote:

> I will only say further that my dearest sister, my tender, watch-
> ful, indefatigable nurse, has not been made ill by her exertions.
> As to what I owe to her, and to the anxious affection of all my
> beloved family on this occasion, I can only cry over it, and pray
> for God to bless them more and more.[21]

In *Persuasion*, the heroine Anne Elliot attributed the fact that
she had become prematurely 'faded', 'thin', and 'haggard', to a
failed romance. This implies that Jane may well have done the
same. In fact, the real cause of Jane's debility lay elsewhere, as
will soon be seen. As for Anne, her bloom returned once more
when she was assured of the true love of Captain Wentworth.

❦ 22 ❦

Jane's Mystery Illness
Explained

In 1964 an article appeared in the *British Medical Journal* entitled 'Jane Austen's Illness' by Sir Vincent Zachary Cope, Consulting Surgeon to St Mary's Hospital, Paddington, London. Jane died, said Cope,

> from an ailment the nature of which has never been ascertained, or, so far as I am aware, seriously discussed. No information was furnished by the doctors who attended her, and her relatives were reticent about her illness, so that we are compelled to rely chiefly on the few comments made by the patient herself in the letters that have survived. Fortunately Jane Austen was an accurate observer, and though she made light of her troubles until near the end one can rely on her definite statements.

By perusing Jane's letters and those of her family, Cope set about attempting to identify the illness that prematurely terminated Jane's life. Of the symptoms suffered by Jane, Cope concludes that whereas many of them might be accounted for by a number of disease conditions, there are very few disease conditions which could account for them all.

Cope describes how he read Jane's letter to Fanny Knight of 23/25 March 1817, many times before it struck him that in her use of the words, 'recovering my looks a little, which have been bad enough, black and white and every wrong colour', she was describing 'that symptom which is almost pathognomonic of

Addison's disease'. Cope goes on to explain that this appearance is due to pigmented areas of the skin mingling with non-pigmented areas. There is no disease other than Addison's disease, he says, that could produce a face that was 'black and white' and at the same time give rise to the other symptoms described in her letters.[1]

Addison's disease is named after the person who first described it: English physician Dr Thomas Addison (1793–1860) of Guy's Hospital who, in 1855, published an important work on *The Constitutional and Local Effects of Diseases of the Suprarenal Capsules* (now commonly known as the adrenal glands). He summarised the main features of the disease as follows:

> The leading and characteristic features of the morbid state to which I would draw attention are: anaemia, general languor and debility, remarkable feebleness of the heart's action, irritability of the stomach and a peculiar change of colour in the skin.

It should also be noted that this is a rare disease; the onset of which is insidious. From time to time there may be severe attacks of nausea, vomiting or diarrhoea. Pigmentation of the skin only occurs late on in the disease and gradually increases – its colour ranging from a bronzy yellow to brown, or even occasionally black. This shows itself, particularly, over exposed parts of the body, such as the face and hands, and wherever prolonged pressure is applied to the skin, such as beneath a waist belt and, occasionally, on mucous membranes as in the mouth. The patient's temperature is usually, somewhat subnormal.[2]

Although Addison's disease was not described until after Jane Austen's time, it is now known to be caused by a malfunction of the adrenal glands (one of which is situated above each kidney) which normally produce the so-called corticosteroid hormones – hydrocortisone and aldosterone. A deficiency of the above hormones, which is found in Addison's disease, causes the pituitary gland to react by secreting excessive amounts of adrenocorticotrophic hormone (ACTH), and also of melanocyte stimulating hormone (MSH). It is the latter which causes the skin to increase its production of melanin pigments – hence the excessive pigmentation.

Another feature of Addison's disease is the occurrence, at intervals, of so-called Addisonian crises which occur due to the failure of the adrenal glands to produce corticosteroid hormones, which normally help the body to cope with stress. In the Addisonian crisis, the patient develops extreme muscle-wasting, becomes dehydrated, confused and comatose. He or she also suffers from hypotension (low blood pressure) and often hypoglycaemia (a deficiency of sugar in the blood). As Addison's disease progresses to the chronic stage, the patient becomes tired, weak and suffers with vague abdominal pains and weight loss.[3] This begs the question, what causes the adrenal glands to fail?

Samuel Wilks, a pupil of Addison's and also his co-worker, declared that Addison's disease was always caused by the suprarenal capsules (adrenal glands) becoming infected with tuberculosis – an infectious disease caused by the bacterium Mycobacterium tuberculosis. Tuberculosis is passed from person to person in airborne droplets, by coughs and sneezes, and it can also be contracted by drinking the milk of tuberculous cattle. The disease, in this latter case, is caused by a similar organism, Mycobacterium bovis.

Tuberculosis commonly begins with the infection of one organ of the body at a so-called primary site. Following this, the infected person will either go on to develop immunity, or the disease will spread to other secondary sites. Any organ of the body may be infected: the commonest being lungs, intestines, bones and glands. (Incidentally, Jane's great-grandfather John Austen died of 'consumption' in 1704 – consumption being an early name for tuberculosis, a disease which appears to consume the body).

In 1911 (when the incidence of tuberculosis among the population was probably little different from what it had been in Jane Austen's time), an article on Addison's disease in the *Encyclopaedia Britannica* read as follows:

> The morbid anatomy [anatomy of diseased organs] shows that in over 80% of the cases . . . the changes in the suprarenals [adrenal glands] are those due to tuberculosis, usually beginning in the medulla [central region of the gland] and resulting in more or less caseation [the destruction of the organ by its conversion into a cheese-like material].

(Note that this figure of 80% is somewhat lower than Wilks's 100%.)

> . . . that this lesion is bilateral [i.e. affects the adrenal glands on both the right and the left side] and usually secondary to tuberculous disease elsewhere, especially of the spinal column.

It seems more than likely, therefore, that Jane was suffering from tuberculosis, and that this is what had destroyed her adrenal glands. This would explain her night fevers – a typical symptom of tuberculosis (but not of Addison's disease). Also, if tuberculosis was present in her spinal column which, from the above statement, seems likely, then this could account for the backache of which she complained – this symptom again being atypical of Addison's disease. How, therefore, did Jane contract tuberculosis?

THE PREVALENCE OF TUBERCULOSIS

In early nineteenth-century England, it is estimated that a quarter of all deaths were due to tuberculosis, and the following examples, which were known to Jane, reveal just how prevalent it was. In November 1798 Jane described how Anna Lefroy had seen 'a great deal of the Mapletons while she was in Bath', David Mapleton being a surgeon-apothecary in that city. The Mapletons had a 17-year-old son, of whom Jane remarked: 'Christian is still in a very bad state of health, consumptive [tubercular] and not likely to recover'.[4] In fact, Christian lived on until 1839. On 12–13 May 1801, Jane declared, in respect of 22-year-old Marianne Mapleton, sister of Christian, 'I am always told that she is better . . . Her complaint is billious fever'.[5] However, shortly afterwards, Jane recorded that Marianne's disorder had 'ended fatally'.[6] So had Marianne also contracted tuberculosis?

Further evidence that the disease was rife in the community in which Jane lived is born out by Mrs Lefroy, who in June 1801, described how her husband had recently visited one James Corbett, who was 'in a deep consumption'.[7]

Jane herself may have contracted tuberculosis from infected milk or other dairy produce, or she may have contracted it via droplet infection through a chance encounter with an infected stranger. However, it is more likely that she caught it from another member of her family, namely her brother Henry.

HENRY AUSTEN

As long ago as 29 October 1801, Henry's wife Eliza had written to her cousin Phylly expressing concern about her husband who for five months never enjoyed an hour's health – His complaints were a Cough, Hectic pain in the side and in short every thing which denotes a galloping consumption [a rapidly spreading form of tuberculosis] in which I believe all his acquaintance thought him.[8]

On 3 November 1813 Jane wrote to Cassandra about Henry, who had not been well. She wrote that Henry's

... illness & the dull time of year together make me feel that it would be horrible of me not to offer to remain with him [i.e. at his home in London] – & therefore, unless you know of any objection, I wish you would tell him with my best Love that I shall be most happy to spend 10 days or a fortnight at Henrietta St [where he now lived] – if he will accept me.[9]

Three days later, Jane wrote again to Cassandra: 'Dearest Henry! What a turn he has for being ill! & what a thing Bile is!'[10] In other words, Henry's symptoms and Jane's were similar in this respect.

Henry's health did not improve, for Jane's niece Caroline described how, in the autumn of 1815, when Jane was visiting him at his house, now Hans Place, London, 'He was seized with a low fever and became so ill that his life was despaired of'.[11] He survived, however, and was nursed for some weeks by Jane. On 17 October of that year Jane herself stated that Henry was 'not quite well' and suffering from 'a bilious attack with fever'.[12] This fever was still present when Jane wrote to Cassandra again the following month. In his *Memoir*, James E. Austen-Leigh describes Henry's fever as 'dangerous' and his convalescence from it as, 'slow'.[13] As already mentioned, fever, especially at night, is a symptom of tuberculosis, as are 'bilious attacks'.

It seems likely, therefore, that Henry was suffering from tuberculosis and that Jane contracted it from him. After all, she had nursed her brother for several weeks and it is known that the longer a person is exposed to someone with tuberculosis, the more likely he or she is to become infected. Jane had been in close and prolonged contact with Henry since the autumn of 1815. Her own symptoms had commenced at the beginning of the following year 1816. This correlates with the average incubation period for tuberculosis being twenty weeks, though it can be as short as two weeks.[14]

If Henry did indeed have tuberculosis, why did he not succumb to the disease? The answer is that the body reacts to an attack of tuberculosis by enclosing the infected area in fibrous tissue, which has the effect of preventing the spread of the infection. (If the bacteria leak out then the infection may spread). Whatever the truth of the matter may be, Henry survived and lived to the age of 78.

EDWARD (AUSTEN) KNIGHT

Jane's brother Edward, was another member of the family who suffered poor health, and on 24/25 December 1798, Jane wrote to Cassandra about him thus:

> I hope with the assistance of Bowel complaints, Faintnesses & Sicknesses, he will soon be restored to that Blessing likewise. – If his nervous complaint proceeded from a suppression of something that ought to be thrown out ... the first of these Disorders may really be a remedy, & I sincerely wish it may ...[15]

In other words, Jane believed that it was necessary for Edward to endure the above symptoms, prior to him recovering.

On 2 June 1799 Jane wrote to Cassandra from Bath, indicating that Edward's health was still not good:

> What must I tell you of Edward? – Truth or Falsehood? – I will try the former, & you may chuse for yourself another time. – He was better yesterday than he had been for two or three days before, about as well as while he was at Steventon that he drinks at the Hetling Pump [which derived its water from the Hetling spring], is to bathe tomorrow, & try Electricity [or 'galvanisation', medical treatment whereby a pulse of electric current is used to stimulate the contraction of the muscles of the body] on Tuesday.[16]

About a week later Jane reported that:

> Edward had been pretty well for this last Week, & as the Waters have never disagreed with him in any respect, We are inclined to hope that he will derive advantage from them in the end …[17]

However, by 19 June the situation had changed:

> Edward has not been well these last two days; his appetite has failed him, & he has complained of sick & uncomfortable feelings, which with other Symptoms make us think of the Gout.[18]

What was the cause of Edward's illness? The following remarks by Jane indicate that even his doctor did not know. She said:

> [Edward] attributes his present little feverish indisposition to his having ate something unsuited to his Stomach – I do not understand that Mr Anderton [Edward Anderdon, apothecary of Queen's Square, Bath] suspects the Gout at all.[19]

Edward was clearly suffering from a chronic illness. His symptoms of sickness, poor appetite, bowel complaints and faintness indicate that he, too, may have been suffering from tuberculosis.

MRS CASSANDRA AUSTEN

In October 1798 Jane described how, after a journey, her mother 'was a good deal indisposed from that particular kind of evacuation [presumably an emptying of the bowels] which had generally preceded her Illnesses'. Also, that she had 'felt a heat in her throat as we travelled yesterday morning, which seemed to foretell more Bile'.[20]

In December Jane stated that Mr John Lyford, surgeon of Winchester, had called the previous day, dined with the Austens and expressed the wish for 'my mother to look yellow and to throw out a rash, but she will do neither'. The doctor appeared to have been looking for some tangible signs that would enable him to make the diagnosis, but he was unable to find them.[21]

Later that month Jane reported to Cassandra:

My Mother continues hearty, her appetite & nights are very good, but her Bowels are still not entirely settled, & she sometimes complains of an Asthma, a Dropsy [oedema – accumulation of fluid, most commonly in the lower legs], Water in her Chest & a Liver Disorder.[22]

In the case of Mrs Austen, the presence of bilious attacks and bowel disorder is in keeping with the symptoms of tuberculosis. However, the presence of oedema, the fact that her appetite was good, and the lack of mention of fever or night sweats suggests some other, unknown disease (though co-existing tuberculosis cannot be totally ruled out).

JAMES AUSTEN

A poem written by Jane's eldest brother James, entitled 'Lines written at Steventon in the Autumn of 1814' when he was aged 49, reveals a man who considered himself to be 'an invalid' who lived in 'sad seclusion', and which speaks sorrowfully of 'what remains/Of my allotted time . . .'[23] It is not known from what ailment James was suffering, or whether, prior to this time, he had been in the company of his brother Henry, who presumably was tubercular. Whatever it was that James was suffering from he, in his poem, 'mocks the healing power/Of any medicine, but his native air'. James also was correct in believing that his life would not be a long one; he died in December 1819 aged 54.

CAROLINE AUSTEN

In 1815, the year after her father wrote the above poem alluding to the fact that he was far from well, his daughter Caroline, then aged 9, stated: 'In the May of this year I had an illness such as was then called bilious fever. Soon after I recovered . . .'[24] This, as already mentioned, is a symptom typical of tuberculosis (but of course not diagnostic of that condition). If Caroline's symptoms were the result of a tubercular infection, it may be assumed that she developed an immunity to that disease, for she lived to be 75.

How ironic it is that in the fourteenth letter of Jane's *Love and Freindship* – from her *Juvenilia* – Laura describes the terminal illness of her friend Sophia as follows:

Her disorder turned to a galloping Consumption and in a few Days carried her off. Amidst all my Lamentations for her (and violent you may suppose they were), I yet received some consolation in the reflection of my having paid every Attention to her that could be offered, in her illness.

As for Sophia, her last words to Laura were:

Beware of fainting fits . . . Though at the time they may be refreshing and agreable yet beleive me they will in the end, if too often repeated and at improper seasons, prove destructive to your Constitution . . . Run mad as often as you chuse, but do not faint.[25]

✿ 23 ✿

Sanditon

Jane's last (and unfinished) novel *Sanditon* was written between 27 January and 18 March 1817, by which time her health had deteriorated alarmingly. (It was not published until 1925). At that time, there was a school of thought, which Jane was aware of, to the effect that sea water and sea air had curative or restorative properties. It is no coincidence, therefore, that the book's setting is the fictitious town of Sanditon, described as 'a young and rising bathing-place, which everybody has heard of'. By contrast, the story also implies that the medical profession is, as often as not, ineffectual when it comes to the treatment of disease. In fact, the novel begins with an immediate attack on that profession.

Mr Parker and his wife are travelling along the coast road near Tonbridge in Kent, when their coach overturns in a rough lane, in the course of which Mr Parker sprains his ankle. The accident has been seen by local man Mr Heywood who, when asked if there is a surgeon nearby replies: 'The surgeon sir! I'm afraid you'll find no surgeon at hand here, but I dare say we shall do very well without him'.

When Lady Denham of Sanditon hears that Parker has requested a doctor, she is equally scathing about the medical profession:

Going after a doctor! – Why, what should we do with a doctor here? It would be only encouraging our servants and the poor to fancy themselves ill, if there was a doctor at hand – Oh! pray, let us have none of the tribe at Sanditon. We go on very well as we are. Here have I lived seventy good years in the world and never took physic above twice – and never saw the face of a doctor in all my life, on my own account. – And I verily believe if my poor dear [late husband] Sir Harry had never seen one neither, he would have been alive now. – Ten fees, one after another, did the man take who sent him out of the world. – I beseech you Mr Parker, no doctors here.

Parker, who owns land and property in the parish of Sanditon, declares that he is enthusiastic about popularising the resort with a view to its future development and expansion. He relishes the prospect of changing it from 'a quiet village of no pretentions' to 'a profitable speculation'. (This was the second reason, apart from his sprained ankle, why Parker had attempted to locate a surgeon, for if he could establish such a person in Sanditon, then 'the advantage of [having] a medical man at hand would very materially promote the rise and prosperity of the place').

It was Parker's view that:

No person could be really well, no person could be really in a state of secure and permanent health without spending at least six weeks by the sea every year. – The sea air and sea bathing together were nearly infallible, one or other of them being a match for every disorder, of the stomach, the lungs or the blood; they were anti-spasmodic, anti-pulmonary, anti-sceptic, anti-bilious and anti-rheumatic.

Heywood, however, takes the opposite view, saying that if the moneyed classes were to be attracted to Sanditon, this would be 'sure to raise the price of provisions and make the poor good for nothing [i.e. purposeless]'. In fact, he thought that the coastline was already 'too full of them [such resorts] altogether'.

The story so far shows that the author was aware that the traditional ways of life, particularly those of the country, were fast disappearing. For example, it was said of Heywood, who was a traditionalist, that:

> Excepting two journeys to London in the year, to receive his dividends, [he] went no farther than his feet or his well-tried old horse could carry him, and Mrs Heywood's adventurings were only now or then to visit her neighbours, in the old coach which had been new when they were married and fresh lined on their eldest son's coming of age ten years ago.

In contrast the new world, as epitomised by Parker, was one where commerce and trade were all important.

Parker was anxious that Mr and Mrs Heywood should visit Sanditon, but he could not prevail upon them to do so. However, they did agree that their eldest daughter, Miss Charlotte Heywood, might accompany the Parkers back to Sanditon.

Parker has two sisters, Susan and Diana, and a brother Arthur. In reference to his sisters, Parker declares:

> They have wretched health . . . and are subject to a variety of very serious disorders. Indeed, I do not believe they know what a day's health is.

On the other hand, he also admits that 'there is a good deal of imagination' in them. Likewise, Parker's youngest brother Arthur, who lives with the sisters, was 'almost as great an invalid as themselves'.

When Diana writes to her brother Parker, the latter imagines what his other brother Sidney would say if he could see her letter:

> I know he would be offering odds, that either Susan, Diana or Arthur would appear by this letter to have been at the point of death within the last month.

Sure enough, in the letter, Diana refers to having had 'a more severe attack than usual of my old grievance, spasmodic bile and hardly able to crawl from my bed to the sofa'. And in a swipe at the medical profession, she declares:

> We have entirely done with the whole medical tribe. We have consulted physician after physician in vain, till we are quite convinced that they can do nothing for us and that we must trust to our own knowledge of our own wretched constitutions for any relief.

Here, Jane is living vicariously through Diana, whose symptoms of biliousness, together with weakness which obliges her to lie on the sofa, are identical to her own. However, whereas Diana is neurotic and complaining, Jane by contrast, is courageous and stoical.

Diana's sister Susan is, according to the former, in an equally unfortunate predicament:

> She has been suffering much from the headache ... and the proposed remedy of six leeches a day for ten days together relieved her so little that we thought it right to change our measures.

It is then decided that the 'evil lay in her [Susan's] gum', and accordingly it was arranged that she should have three teeth extracted. This made her 'decidedly better' but on the other hand her nerves were still 'a good deal deranged'.

Despite their tendency to hypochondria, Parker took a charitable view of his sisters, and in spite of all their sufferings he declared them to be much 'occupied in promoting the good of others!' (This is Jane, as usual, seeing some good in everybody).

Arthur and his sisters duly arrive in Sanditon, take lodgings in the town and are introduced to Charlotte Heywood, who is sceptical about their alleged sufferings. In regard to Diana, for instance,

> [she] could perceive no symptoms of illness which she [Charlotte], in the boldness of her own good health, would not have undertaken to cure, by putting out the fire, opening the window, and disposing of the drops and the salts [with which she plied herself] . . .

As for Diana's brother Arthur, it was Charlotte's opinion that his 'enjoyments in invalidism were very different from his sister's', and also that he was inclined to use his alleged illnesses to his advantage, being 'determined on having no disorders but such as called for warm rooms and good nourishment'.

Towards the end of *Sanditon* a Miss Lambe appears, who is sick and 'under the constant care of an experienced physician'. Perhaps, had Jane Austen been able to complete the story, there would have been friction between this lady, who appears to have had a serious health complaint, and Susan, Diana and Arthur Parker, who undoubtedly did not.

As regards the obvious hostility shown towards the medical profession in the novel *Sanditon*, it should be remembered that its author Jane was in poor and rapidly deteriorating health herself when she wrote it. Her doctors were unable to cure her, and it is only natural that she should have lashed out at their perceived ignorance and incompetence. On the other hand, to be fair to the doctors, Jane was suffering coincidentally from not one, but two diseases. The first was Addison's disease, which was unknown to them at the time. The second (as has been demonstrated beyond reasonable doubt) was tuberculosis, for which, in those days, there was no known cure.

Likewise, a person such as Jane who was genuinely sick – and she must have felt dreadfully unwell as the combined effects of these two diseases gradually overcame her – would not take kindly to those who feign or exaggerate their illnesses. Therefore, not only did she portray her characters Susan, Diana and Arthur as figures of fun, she also shows a thinly disguised contempt for them as she scorns their constant whinging and play-acting. The message of Sanditon is this: if you are ill, then try to bear your illness bravely, which, by all accounts, is what Jane herself did.

In early 1817, Edward's daughter Fanny consulted Jane, once again, over her (Fanny's) love life. Should she have accepted Mr John Plumptre, who was now courting another lady? Was she, at the age of only 24, in imminent danger of being left on the shelf? She goes on to ask Jane her opinion of another suitor, Mr Wildman. (Fanny eventually married Sir Edward Knatchbull, Bt, in 1820).

✧ 24 ✧

The Death of Jane Austen

Jane Austen died at 4.30 a.m. on 18 July 1817 at the age of 41. It was left to Jane's sister Cassandra to describe the last few hours of her life which, in a letter to her niece Fanny Knight, she did in a most moving way:

> . . . on Thursday I went into the Town to do an errand your dear Aunt was anxious about. I returnd about a quarter before six & found her recovering from faintness & oppression, she got so well as to be able to give me a minute account of her seizure & when the clock struck 6 she was talking quietly to me. I cannot say how soon afterwards she was seized again with the same faintness, which was followed by the sufferings she could not describe, but Mr Lydford had been sent for, had applied something to give her ease & she was in a state of quiet insensibility by seven oclock at the latest. From that time till half past four when she ceased to breathe, she scarcely moved a limb . . .[1]

Jane's funeral was attended by only a handful of mourners, including three of her brothers: Edward, Henry and Francis. James did not attend, but sent his son James E. Austen-Leigh in his place. The reason was, according to the latter's sister Caroline, that:

> in the sad state of his own [James senior's] health and nerves, the trial would be too much for him. He therefore stayed at home.[2]

Caroline also stated that:

> Capt. Charles Austen is not named amongst those who came
> to Winchester & I make [I am] sure he must then have been at
> sea – or he would certainly have been amongst the mourners.[3]

The funeral was arranged by Henry and conducted by the
Revd Thomas Watkins, precentor of the cathedral. It was held
early in the morning to avoid clashing with Morning Prayers
at 10 o'clock. Women were not expected to attend funerals and
Cassandra's last sight of the coffin was when it left 8, College
Street.

Two days after Jane's death, Cassandra wrote to her niece
Fanny Knight:

> I have lost a treasure, such a Sister, such a friend as never can
> have been surpassed, – She was the sun of my life, the gilder of
> every pleasure, the soother of every sorrow . . . & it is as if I had
> lost a part of myself.

However, Cassandra goes on to say:

> You know me too well to be at all afraid that I should suffer
> materially from my feelings, I am perfectly conscious of the
> extent of my irreparable loss, but I am not at all overpowered &
> very little indisposed, nothing but what a short time, with rest
> & change of air will remove.

In other words, yes, my sister has died, but I shall soon get over
it. How strongly this contrasts with Jane's sentiments when she
lost her dearest friend Mrs Lefroy, and four years later wrote a
moving poem in her memory. There follows an even stranger
statement from Cassandra:

I thank God that I was enabled to attend to her to the last & amongst my many causes of self-reproach I have not to add any wilfull neglect of her comfort.[4]

So what were these 'many causes of self-reproach'? Did Cassandra feel that in some way during the course of Jane's final illness, she had neglected her sister? Or was it something else that she felt guilty about; something far more profound; something, perhaps, that related to Jane's love affair in Devonshire all those years ago in the summer of 1802?

On 29 July 1817, when Cassandra wrote again to Fanny, it is clear that once again her concern is principally for herself:

I continue tolerably well – much better than anyone could have supposed possible, because I certainly have had considerable fatigue of body as well as anguish of mind for months back; but I really am well, and I hope I am properly grateful to the Almighty for having been so supported.[5]

In her will, Jane left everything to her sister Cassandra, apart from a legacy of £50 to her brother Henry, and £50 to Mme Bigeon – Henry's former housekeeper; the residue of her estate being £561.2s 0d. Martha Lloyd received Jane's topaz cross which had been given to her by her brother Charles.

After Jane's death, her brother Henry, whom she had named as her literary executor, oversaw the publication of *Northanger Abbey* (previously *Susan*) and *Persuasion*, both by John Murray in December 1817 (dated 1818).

☙ 25 ☙

Epilogue

In many ways, Jane Austen was a woman of the twentieth or twenty-first centuries (rather than of the nineteenth), in that she found a great deal that was archaic and ridiculous about the society in which she found herself: its manners, its customs, its traditions, its prejudices. Equally, this provided a great deal of material for her to satirise and, in doing so, employed all those tools of the satirist's trade – irony, sarcasm, invective, wit, parody, mockery, humour – as a means for achieving her ends. However, those features of middle-class, nineteenth-century life which she did admire, such as good manners, smartness of appearance and traditional family values of love and friendship (which was the title of one of her books), she embraced wholeheartedly.

The influence of Jane's cousin Eliza, which in the past has been underestimated, has been discussed. The similarity of their humour has been remarked upon, and of their style of writing. Also, Eliza encouraged Jane with her French and her music and singing, and taught her manners and social graces. But as already mentioned, there are elements of Eliza's character with which Jane would certainly not have approved.

In *Northanger Abbey* Jane parodies the Gothic novel. In *A History of England* she parodies the dry, dull, formal historical textbooks of the day. In *Persuasion* she makes a burlesque of Sir Walter Elliot who, she declares, had never read any book but *The Baronetage* and to whom vanity was the 'beginning and end' of his character. In *Pride and Prejudice*, through her hero-ine Elizabeth Bennet, she mocks Mr Darcy for his insufferable pride and for the way he regards Elizabeth and her connec-tions as being inferior.

The satirist may also be accused of being destructive; criti-cal and dissatisfied with everything that he or she encounters, while at the same time having nothing positive to put in its place. This is certainly not the case with Jane. Her heroines know exactly what they want from their husbands-to-be, and are quite capable of using satire as a weapon in order to make such prospective husbands more amenable and turn them into better people. Elizabeth Bennet used this technique to great effect, both against Darcy's pride and against his prejudices. Nevertheless, in a society which was deeply class conscious, a certain amount of courage is required from Jane's heroines if they are to make their voices heard. An example of this is the way Elizabeth Bennet stands up to the opinionated and insuf-ferable Lady Catherine de Bourgh.

From the words and deeds of Jane's heroines one may deduce that she, herself, was fiercely egalitarian. She felt strongly that people should be judged on their merits of char-acter, judgement and education, rather than on what their connections were or how many thousand a year was going into their bank accounts. Also, there is a deep, underlying humanity in the novels, for example, in the solicitous way in which Mr Woodhouse shows concern for his daughter Emma, who reciprocates by showing her concern for him. Again, one may deduce that courage and humanity were also a part of Jane's make-up.

When a character is found to be wanting, such as Mr Wickham (*in Pride and Prejudice*), who elopes with Mrs Bennet's daughter Lydia, Jane does not seek to humiliate and destroy him. There is no spiteful and retributive destruction of the miscreant on the part of Jane the author. Instead, matters are usually resolved in a civilised manner and the offender is allowed to retain some dignity.

Jane's ability to see the humorous side of a situation permits the present-day reader to look back at her life and times, and at those of her contemporaries, in the same light-hearted way; rather than judging and, perhaps, condemning them by the standards of today.

In her early life Jane was dependent on a small allowance made to her by her father George, who himself was obliged to take in pupils in order to supplement his modest income. This, as Jane's letters indicate, meant that she was always obliged to live frugally. From the time of her father's death in 1805, Jane's position became worse in that her family became reliant on the charity of her brothers; in particular Francis, who accommodated them at his home in Southampton, and Edward who found them a home at Chawton. Only latterly did the income from her books provide Jane with what she herself would have described as a 'modest competence'. How she must have longed for the security, which in happier circumstances, a loving husband of even modest means might have provided.

Jane, undoubtedly, lived vicariously through her heroines and relished the moment when they could find the right man, marry and live happily ever after. How sad that in her life, despite the fact that she had a number of romances, she was never able to achieve such a state of marital bliss as she effected for the likes of Elizabeth Bennet and Emma Woodhouse. Instead, with her final illness which caused not only pain but disfigurement, she knew that her last chance of happiness had gone. Yet, with her wonderfully creative spirit she carried on writing in the same satirical and witty way that she had always done, this time choosing, in *Sanditon*, to satirise groups of neurotic people who could produce medical ailments at the drop of a hat.

The many aspects of Jane's personality and life continue to intrigue to this day:

HER STRENGTH OF CHARACTER

It would be a mistake to think of Jane as a weak and sentimental person. She was well able to stand up for herself as, for instance, when the Austens relocated from Steventon to Bath, and she felt that her siblings were helping themselves to more of their fair share of the family's possessions. And why should she not have done so? 'Stoical' is an epithet which may rightly be applied to Jane, and yet occasionally, the mask slips and she reveals her vulnerabilities as, for example, when she admits to weeping at the departure of her early love, Tom Lefroy.

HER ABILITY TO FORGIVE

This was one of Jane's most remarkable qualities. She demonstrates it not only in her novels, but also in real life, in respect of Mrs Lefroy and also her sister Cassandra. A good example is found in *Pride and Prejudice*, where Elizabeth Bennet is willing to be reconciled to Wickham even though the latter has previously brought disgrace on the family by eloping with her sister Lydia.

HER RELATIONSHIP WITH CASSANDRA

This was not always one of sweetness and light. In her letters Jane harangues her sister for failing, in her eyes, to be a good correspondent, and also for failing to be there when Jane needed her.

In her novel *The Watsons*, Jane chooses to deal, in an unchar-
acteristically immoderate, even bitter way, with the subject of
sisterly betrayal. Her poem entitled 'Miss Austen', discovered
by Lord Brabourne in 1807, is about love and it refers to those
who were once friends becoming bitter foes. Also, the fact
that after the title Jane has included Cassandra's name – written in brackets – implies that Jane intends the sentiments
which she expressed therein, to be directed towards her sister.
Finally, Cassandra's phrase, 'my many causes of self-reproach',
was written in respect of Jane after her death. These coded
signals appear to reveal that the sisters had a falling out and
that one, presumably Cassandra, betrayed the other, in an affair
of the heart.

HER MYSTERIOUS LOVER

Until now, the identity of Jane's Devonshire lover has remained
a mystery, largely because Cassandra destroyed those letters of
Jane's which might have shed light on the subject. Cassandra
did, however, admit both to her niece Caroline and to her
niece Anna, that the man's name was Blackall. Evidence has
been put forward that this lover was, in fact, the Revd Samuel
Blackall, the same gentleman whom Jane had met (at Mrs
Lefroy's instigation) in 1798. The evidence for this, although
circumstantial, is strong:

Firstly, we have Cassandra's word that his name was Blackall.
Secondly, we know he was visiting his brother who was a
doctor in South Devonshire. Thirdly, we know that the Austens
paid a visit to South Devonshire, and more particularly to the
vicinity in which Dr John Blackall practised medicine, in the
summer of 1802. What clinches the matter is the fact that,
according to parish records, Samuel Blackall is known to have

had a younger brother, Dr John Blackall, who was practising in Devon at the time.

CASSANDRA'S ROLE

Why did Cassandra choose to destroy the evidence relating to Blackall, but not that which related to another gentleman with whom Jane fell in love, namely Tom Lefroy? If Cassandra did indeed attempt to steal Blackall from Jane, as both *The Watsons* and the poem 'Miss Austen' appear to imply, and if Jane had alluded to this in her letters, then surely this would have given Cassandra a motive to destroy them. After all, had their contents become known to the family, or to the public at large, Cassandra would have been portrayed in a very poor light indeed. Also, the time frame fits perfectly in that the 'missing letter' period encompasses the year 1802, when Jane and Blackall were reunited.

That Cassandra was mightily impressed by Blackall is born out by Caroline Austen in her (previously mentioned) letter to Mary Leigh. Caroline states that when she, her mother and Cassandra 'made the acquaintance of a certain Mr. Henry Eldridge of the Engineers', Cassandra said that this gentleman, whom she regarded as 'very pleasing', 'good looking', 'unusually gifted' and 'agreeable', reminded her of the gentleman 'whom they had met one Summer when they were by the sea'.

Alternatively, is it possible that Cassandra – and not Jane – was the victim, and that it was the former to whom Blackall was attracted? This is unlikely, for if Jane was the culprit then why was she so anxious to emphasise the subject of sisterly betrayal, both in *The Watsons* and in her poem?

THE OUTCOME

Did Blackall keep in touch with Jane during the 'missing letter' years, and if so, why did he not propose to her (instead of to Susannah Lewis) when he finally obtained his Somersetshire living and became Rector of Great Cadbury in 1812? After all, Jane, at that time was in good health, her final illnesses not yet having manifested themselves. This question remains unanswered.

THE CESSATION OF JANE'S NOVEL-WRITING

In 1804 Jane lost her dear friend Mrs Lefroy, and in 1805 she lost her beloved father George. It also seems to be the case that in 1802 she had experienced the trauma of a failed relationship with Blackall. If, in addition, there was a simultaneous breakdown in Jane's relationship with her, hitherto, beloved sister Cassandra whom she adored, this may explain why her novel-writing virtually ceased for over a decade (from 1798 to 1810).

Reading between the lines, it appears that Jane convinced herself that her sister had influenced Blackall against her, and tried to steal him for herself. There is, however, another interpretation of events. In meeting with the Austen family again in 1802, was Blackall merely attempting, in his words, to improve his 'acquaintance with that family', rather than with one of its members in particular – i.e. either Jane or Cassandra? Had Jane misread the signs, believing him to be in love with her when he was not? And when this became obvious, did she turn, unfairly, on her sister and apportion blame for the failed relationship to her? There is evidence that Jane sometimes did get matters out of proportion as far as Cassandra was concerned; she scolded her, for example, when the latter failed to write to her, or was absent from home for what she considered to be inordinately long periods of time; times when Cassandra clearly desired some life of her own.

HER FINAL ILLNESS

The mystery relating to Jane's final illness was largely solved by physician Sir Zachary Cope in 1964, when he diagnosed her condition as Addison's disease. This, however, was only part of Jane's problem for, as has been demonstrated, it is highly likely that she was also suffering from tuberculosis of the spine – a disease which she appears to have contracted from her brother Henry while she was nursing him.

Jane's novels portray middle and upper-class society, where the characters, in the main, occupy fine houses, walk about in fine clothes and stroll leisurely through idyllic gardens and parks. Her characters – even the bad ones – almost invariably live happily ever after, in an environment where poverty and sickness figure only peripherally.

How can it be that Jane, all too often, sees misfortune and even death as an opportunity for humour? This, undoubtedly, was for her a coping mechanism; one which enabled her to avoid facing up to the more unpleasant side of life. And yet, in her novels, she demonstrates her concern for the wronged and underprivileged on countless occasions: in *Mansfield Park*, where Fanny Price is denied a fire in her bedroom; in *Emma*, where Emma Woodhouse insults Miss Bates; in *Sense and Sensibility*, where Sir John Middleton takes pity on the Dashwood family after they find themselves homeless. Neither should it be forgotten that Jane looked after her mother – a chronically sick woman – for many years without complaint, and devotedly nursed her brother Henry when he too became ill.

'I consider everybody as having the right to marry once in their Lives for Love, if they can . . .'[1] These words were written by Jane to her sister Cassandra in 1808. They undoubtedly reflect a tremendous regret on her part, that during the years in which she might reasonably have expected to find conjugal happiness, she did not do so. However, in a letter which Jane subsequently wrote to her niece Fanny Knight, she affirmed that being on one's own is preferable to being with the wrong person:

> Nothing can be compared to the misery of being bound without Love, bound to one, & preferring another. That is a Punishment which you do not deserve.[2]

Jane subsequently advised Fanny:

> Do not be in a hurry; depend upon it, the right Man will come at last; you will, in the course of the next two or three years, meet with somebody more generally unexceptionable than anyone you have yet known, who will love you as warmly as ever He [Mr James Wildman] did, & who will so completely attach you, that you will feel you never really loved before.[3]

What if Jane had married and had children of her own? Would she have made a good mother, and enjoyed the experience? This may be deduced from the comments which her nieces and others made about her, and also by what she said about them. Caroline Austen, for example, was the daughter of Jane's eldest brother James by his second wife Mary Lloyd. She was only 12 years old when her Aunt Jane died and therefore 'knew her only with a child's knowledge'. About Jane, Caroline had this to say:

> Her charm to children was great sweetness of manner – she seemed to love you, and you loved her naturally in return – this as well I can now recollect and analyse, was what I felt in my earliest days, before I was old enough to be amused by her cleverness – But soon came the delight of her playful talk – every-thing she could make amusing to a child – Then, as I got older, and when cousins came to share the entertainment, she would tell us the most delightful stories chiefly of fairyland ...
>
> I had taken early to writing verses and stories, and I am sorry to think how I troubled her with reading them. She was very kind about it and always had some praise to bestow.[4]

On another occasion Caroline, whose visits to Chawton were frequent, compared Jane's sister Cassandra with Jane herself – Jane being the one whom she considered to be a warmer and more engaging personality:

> Aunt Jane was a great charm ... I did not dislike Aunt Cassandra – but if my visit had at any time chanced to fall out [occur] during her absence, I don't think I should have missed her – whereas, not to have found Aunt Jane at Chawton, would have been a blank indeed.[5]

James E. Austen-Leigh, Caroline's brother, remarked upon Jane's relationship with her brother (James's uncle) Edward and his children: Though Jane and Edward had been 'a good deal separated' from his family in childhood, 'they were much together in after life, and Jane gave a large share of her affections to him [Edward] and his children'.[6]

Jane was clearly enamoured with her nieces, as this poem which she wrote about Anna Austen typically illustrates:

> In measured verse I'll now rehearse
> The charms of lovely Anna:
> And, first, her mind is unconfined
> Like any vast savannah.

And the poem ends:

> Another world must be unfurled,
> Another language known,
> 'Ere tongue or sound can publish round
> Her charms of flesh and bone.

We are grateful to Jane for leaving us her wonderful portraits of life in a bygone age, albeit for a relatively small and privileged portion of society. Some might view the reading of such works, or the watching of their dramatised re-enactments, as a form of escapism. But what is the harm in that? After all, there are many features of the modern world from which it is a positive relief to escape.

Jane's novels are timeless because they are concerned with human relationships. They demonstrate to us that even today, just as in her day, we have a choice as to what paths we follow, and a duty to differentiate between what is good and what is not – 'goodness' being one of Jane's favourite descriptive words. We rejoice in Jane's gaiety and her wit. We smile at her gentle teasing and dry sarcasm. We salute her courage, and we feel immensely sad that she died so young and that the love – of which she had so much to give to a prospective partner – remained unrequited.

Appendix

STEVENTON RECTORY

Sadly, Steventon Rectory, Jane Austen's birthplace, no longer exists. In 1826–27 Edward Knight built – for the occupation of his son William (Rector of Steventon from 1823–73) – a new rectory on the hillside opposite, overlooking the glebe land's 'Hanging Meadow'. This having been done, he demolished the old one together with its farm buildings and the cottage in the lane. Today, the site of the rectory is indicated by an area where snowdrops grow in springtime, and by the remains of the well from which the Austens obtained their water.

THE CHURCH OF ST NICHOLAS, STEVENTON

It was during William Knight's incumbency that a new spire was added to the church.

In 1936, Jane's great-grandniece Emma Austen-Leigh placed a memorial to Jane on the left-hand side of the nave. In 1952 the fragment of Steventon's Saxon cross was donated to Steventon church by Captain and Mrs Hutton Croft, the then owners of the Steventon Estate. It is now on display inside the church.

Repairs and renovations to the church have been carried out through the generosity of the Jane Austen Societies of

Great Britain and North America. This includes the restoration of the roof and spire (1984), the redecoration of the interior (1988), and the renovation and re-hanging of the church's three medieval bells (1995). In 1975, to mark the bicentenary of Jane's birth, the east window, which suffered from extensive corrosion, was almost entirely replaced. Also, with the help of the Parochial Church Council and Basingstoke and Deane Borough Council, the wrought iron railings surrounding the churchyard were replaced. In 2000, to mark the millennium, a new cover for the font was donated to the church.

STEVENTON MANOR HOUSE

In *c.*1880 Henry Harris, the then owner of the Steventon Estate, built a new manor house which overlooked the original Tudor manor house. Unfortunately, in 1932 this Victorian building, together with an adjacent farm, was destroyed by fire, whereupon the owners, a Mr and Mrs Onslow Fane, decided to extend the Tudor manor house which, sadly, was demolished in 1970.

CHAWTON COTTAGE

Jane's home for the last eight years of her life is now the Jane Austen's House Museum, which has been owned by the Jane Austen Memorial Trust since 1947.

Notes

PREFACE

1. Lord Edward Brabourne, *Letters of Jane Austen*, Vol. II (London: Richard Bentley & Son, 1884), p. 82.
2. Caroline Austen, *My Aunt Jane Austen: A Memoir* (The Jane Austen Society), p. 10.
3. Constance Hill, *Jane Austen: Her Homes and Her Friends* (London: John Lane, 1904), p. 234.
4. Deirdre Le Faye, *Jane Austen's Letters* (Oxford: Oxford University Press, 1997), pp. xv–xvi.

1. STEVENTON: THE CRADLE OF JANE'S GENIUS

1. R.W. Chapman, *Jane Austen: Facts and Problems* (Oxford: Clarendon Press, 1948), p. 20.
2. James E. Austen-Leigh, *A Memoir of Jane Austen* (Oxford: Oxford University, 2002), pp. 23–4, and Chapman, op.cit., p. 21.
3. William Austen-Leigh, *Jane Austen: Her Life and Letters – A Family Record* (London: Smith, Elder & Co., 1913), p. 11.
4. James E. Austen-Leigh, *A Memoir of Jane Austen*, p. 24.

2. JANE'S PARENTS: STEVENTON RECTORY

1. William Austen-Leigh, *Jane Austen: Her Life and Letters*, p. 16.
2. James E. Austen-Leigh, *A Memoir of Jane Austen*, p. 15.
3. Mary Augusta Austen-Leigh, *Personal Aspects of Jane Austen* (Philadelphia: Pavilion Press, 2003), p. 15.
4. William Austen-Leigh, *Jane Austen: Her Life and Letters*, p. 12.
5. R.W. Chapman, *Jane Austen: Facts and Problems*, p. 21.

6. *Ibid.*

7. From an eighteenth-century Terrier, compiled by John Church, Rector of Steventon, 1727–33, and quoted by Deirdre Le Faye in *Jane Austen's Steventon.*

8. Maggie Lane, *We left Bath for Clifton, in Collected Reports of the Jane Austen Society*, Report for 1987.

9. Caroline Austen, *My Aunt Jane Austen*, p. 46.

10. Letter from Jane Austen to Cassandra Austen, 1/2 December 1798.

11. Letter from Jane Austen to Cassandra Austen, 8/9 November 1800.

3. THE YOUNG JANE AUSTEN

1. William Austen-Leigh, *Jane Austen: Her Life and Letters*, p. 22.

2. James E. Austen-Leigh, *A Memoir of Jane Austen*, 1st edition 1869, p. 43.

3. Austen Papers, 28, 29.

4. Anna Lefroy, Lefroy Manuscript, quoted in James E. Austen-Leigh, *A Memoir of Jane Austen*, note 32.

5. Jane Austen Society collected reports, 1976–85, p. 5.

6. R.W. Chapman (ed), *Jane Austen's Letters to her Sister Cassandra* (London: Oxford University Press, 1964), 2nd edition, p. 10.

7. William Austen-Leigh, *Jane Austen: Her Life and Letters*, p. 26.

8. James E. Austen-Leigh, *A Memoir of Jane Austen*, p. 137.

9. William Austen-Leigh, *Jane Austen: Her Life and Letters*, p. 16.

10. Biographical Notice, 1818. *Critical Heritage, 73–8.* In David Nokes, *Jane Austen: A Life* (New York: Farrar, Straus and Giroux, 1997), p. 536.

11. Mary Augusta Austen-Leigh, *Personal Aspects of Jane Austen*, p. 71.

12. Letter from Jane Austen to Cassandra Austen, 18/19 December 1798.

13. James E. Austen-Leigh, *A Memoir of Jane Austen*, p. 157.

14. Letter from Jane Austen to Cassandra Austen, 26 November 1798.

15. James E. Austen-Leigh, *A Memoir of Jane Austen*, p. 158.

4. JANE'S SIBLINGS

1. James E. Austen-Leigh, *A Memoir of Jane Austen*, p. 16.

2. William Austen-Leigh, *Jane Austen: Her Life and Letters*, p. 20.

3. James E. Austen-Leigh, *A Memoir of Jane Austen*, p. 205.

4. Caroline Austen, *My Aunt Jane Austen*, p. 172.

5. Letter from Jane Austen to Cassandra Austen, 25 November 1798.

6. Letter from Jane Austen to Cassandra Austen, 3 January 1799.

7. Le Faye, *Jane Austen's Letters*, p. xv.

8. William Austen-Leigh, *Jane Austen: Her Life and Letters*, p. 49.

9. *Ibid.*, p. 77.

10. *Ibid.*, p. 28.

5. ENTER ELIZA HANCOCK

1. James E. Austen-Leigh, *A Memoir of Jane Austen*, p. 210, note 27.

2. William Austen-Leigh, *Jane Austen: Her Life and Letters*, p. 32.

3. *Ibid.*, p. 10.

4. *Ibid.*

5. William Austen-Leigh, *Jane Austen: Her Life and Letters*, p. 35.

6. Deirdre Le Faye, *Jane Austen's 'Outlandish Cousin'*, (London: The British Library, 2002), p. 46.

7. *Ibid.*, p. 88.

8. William Austen-Leigh, *Jane Austen: Her Life and Letters*, p. 37.

9. *Ibid.*

10. Le Faye, *Jane Austen's 'Outlandish Cousin'*, p. 54.

11. *Ibid.*, p. 55.

12. *Ibid.*, pp. 56–7.

13. *Ibid.*, p. 60.

14. James E. Austen-Leigh, *A Memoir of Jane Austen*, p. 28.

15. *Ibid.*, p. 183.

16. *Ibid.*, p. 28.

6. JANE'S JUVENILIA

1. David Nokes, *Jane Austen: A Life* (New York: Farrar, Straus and Giroux, 1997), p. 96.

2. Letter from Jane Austen to Cassandra Austen, 18 September 1796.

3. Letter from Jane Austen to Cassandra Austen, 1 September 1796.

7. FURTHER ADVENTURES OF ELIZA: HER INFLUENCE ON JANE

1. Le Faye, *Jane Austen's 'Outlandish Cousin'*, p. 76.
2. *Ibid.*, pp. 81–2.
3. *Ibid.*, pp. 80–1.
4. *Ibid.*, pp. 86–7.
5. *Ibid.*, pp. 97–8.
6. *Ibid.*, p. 114.
7. *Ibid.*, p. 116.
8. *Ibid.*, p. 119.
9. Letter from Jane Austen to Cassandra Austen, 16 September 1796.
10. Le Faye, *Jane Austen's 'Outlandish Cousin'*, p. 62.

8. ROMANCE: TOM LEFROY AND EDWARD BRIDGES

1. Letter from Caroline Austen to James E. Austen-Leigh, 1 April 1869, in R.W. Chapman, *Jane Austen's Letters to her Sister Cassandra*, p. 57.
2. Letter from Jane Austen to Cassandra Austen, 17 November 1798.
3. James E. Austen-Leigh, *A Memoir of Jane Austen*, p. 186.
4. Jane Austen Society, *Collected Reports*, 1982, p. 210.
5. Letter from Jane Austen to Cassandra Austen, 5 September 1796.
6. Letter from Jane Austen to Cassandra Austen, 27 August 1805.
7. Letter from Jane Austen to Cassandra Austen, 20 November 1808.
8. Letter from Jane Austen to Cassandra Austen, 26 October 1813.

10. SENSE AND SENSIBILITY

1. Le Faye, *Jane Austen's 'Outlandish Cousin'*, p. 140.

11. THE REVEREND SAMUEL BLACKALL

1. William Austen-Leigh, *Jane Austen: Her Life and Letters*, p. 87.
2. Letter from Jane Austen to Cassandra Austen, 17/18 November 1798.
3. Letter from Jane Austen to Francis Austen, 3/6 July 1813.
4. *Emmanuel College Magazine*, Vol. XLVII (1964–5), p. 44.
5. Letter from Jane Austen to Cassandra Austen, 1/2 December 1798.
6. Letter from Jane Austen to Cassandra Austen, 28 December 1798.
7. James E. Austen-Leigh, *A Memoir of Jane Austen*, p. 17.

8. Letter from Jane Austen to Cassandra Austen, 28 December 1798.
9. Letter from Jane Austen to Cassandra Austen, 24/26 December 1798.
10. Letter from Jane Austen to Cassandra Austen, 18/19 December 1798.

12. NORTHANGER ABBEY

1. J.M. Evans, Jane Austen: Northanger Abbey, p. 10.

13. MORE ABOUT THE FAMILY: THE AUSTENS LEAVE STEVENTON

1. Letter from Jane Austen to Cassandra Austen, 8/9 January 1799.
2. Letter from Jane Austen to Cassandra Austen, 21/23 January 1799.
3. Le Faye, Jane Austen's 'Outlandish Cousin', p. 157.
4. Letter from Jane Austen to Cassandra Austen, 1 November 1800.
5. Letter from Caroline Austen to James E. Austen-Leigh, 1 April 1869(?).
6. Letter from Jane Austen to Cassandra Austen, 3/5 January 1801.
7. Letter from Jane Austen to Cassandra Austen, 8/9 January 1801.
8. Letter from Jane Austen to Cassandra Austen, 21/22 January 1801.
9. Letter from Jane Austen to Cassandra Austen, 26/27 May 1801.
10. Robin Vick, The Sale at Steventon Parsonage, in Jane Austen Society Collected Reports, 1986–95, pp. 295–6.
11. Letter from Jane Austen to Cassandra Austen, 12/13 May 1801.
12. Letter from Jane Austen to Cassandra Austen, 21/22 May 1801.

14. ROMANCE ON THE DEVONSHIRE COAST: A PROPOSAL

OF MARRIAGE

1. Copy of part of a letter from Caroline Austen to James E. Austen-Leigh, National Portrait Gallery, RWC/HH, Folios 8/10 in James E. Austen-Leigh, A Memoir of Jane Austen, pp. 187–8.
2. Chapman, Jane Austen: Facts and Problems, p. 65.
3. Ibid., p.64.
4. Ibid., pp. 67–8.
5. Copy of part of a letter from Catherine Hubback to James E. Austen-Leigh, National Portrait Gallery: A file of correspondence between R.W. Chapman and Henry Hake, 1932–48, RWC/HH,

Folios 11–12 in James E. Austen-Leigh, *A Memoir of Jane Austen*, pp. 191–2. With regard to the identity of Dr Blackall's brother, Catherine Hubback does appear to have been mistaken, in that none of the former's siblings had the name Edward.

6. Letter from Jane Austen to Anna Austen, 10/18 August 1814.

7. Chapman, *Jane Austen: Facts and Problems*, p. 68.

8. P.M.G. Russell, *A History of the Exeter Hospitals, 1170–1948* (Exeter: Exeter Post-Graduate Medical Institute, 1976), p. 47.

9. *Dictionary of National Biography*.

10. Information supplied by Devon County Record Office (from International Genealogical Index) and by the Society of Genealogists.

11. William Austen-Leigh, *Jane Austen: Her Life and Letters*, p.87.

12. *Dictionary of National Biography*.

13. Letter from Catherine Hubback to James E. Austen-Leigh 1 March 1870.

14. Letter from Jane Austen to Cassandra Austen, 7/9 October 1808.

15. Emma Austen-Leigh, *Jane Austen and Lyme Regis* (London: Spottiswoode, Ballantyne and Co., 1946), p. 8.

16. Jane Austen, *Lady Susan, The Watsons and Sanditon* (London: Penguin Books, 2003), p. 184.

15. THE WATSONS

1. Jane Austen, *Lady Susan, The Watsons and Sanditon*, p. 16.

2. Brabourne, *Letters of Jane Austen*, p. 341.

3. Letter from Caroline Austen to James E. Austen-Leigh, National Portrait Gallery, RWC/HH, Folios 8–10.

4. Letter from Catherine Hubback to James E. Austen-Leigh, National Portrait Gallery, RWC/HH, Folios 11–12.

5. Letter from Jane Austen to Francis Austen, 21/22 January 1805.

6. Letter from Jane Austen to Cassandra Austen, 8/11 April 1805.

7. Letter from Jane Austen to Cassandra Austen, 24 August 1805.

8. Letter from Jane Austen to Cassandra Austen, 8/9 February 1807.

9. Letter from Jane Austen to Cassandra Austen, 20/22 February 1807.

10. Letter from Jane Austen to Cassandra Austen, 30 June/1 July 1808.

11. Letter from Jane Austen to Cassandra Austen, 26 June 1808 and 30 June/1 July 1808.

12. Letter from Jane Austen to Cassandra Austen, 13 October 1808.
13. Letter from Jane Austen to Cassandra Austen, 24/25 October 1808.
14. Letter from Jane Austen to Cassandra Austen, 27 December 1808 and 10/11 January 1809.
15. Letter from Jane Austen to Francis Austen, 26 July 1809.
16. Letter from Jane Austen to Cassandra Austen, 18/20 April 1811.

16. MANSFIELD PARK

1. Letter from Jane Austen to Cassandra Austen, 29 January 1813.
2. Letter from Jane Austen to Martha Lloyd, 16 February 1813.
3. The marriage was reported in the *Hampshire Telegraph* of 11 January 1813.
4. Letter from Jane Austen to Francis Austen, 3/6 July 1813.
5. Letter from Jane Austen to Francis Austen, 3 July 1813.
6. Deirdre Le Faye, *Fanny Knight's Diaries* (The Jane Austen Society, 2000), p. 27.
7. Oscar Fay Adams, *The Story of Jane Austen's Life* (USA: Chicago, 1891), p. 176.
8. James E. Austen-Leigh, *A Memoir of Jane Austen*, p. 15.
9. Letter from Jane Austen to Francis Austen, 25 September 1813.
10. Letter from Jane Austen to Cassandra Austen, 14/15 October 1813.
11. Letter from Jane Austen to Anna Austen, 9/18 September 1814.

17. JANE AND ELIZA: TWO OPPOSITES

1. Le Faye, *Jane Austen's 'Outlandish Cousin'*, p. 173.
2. *Ibid.*, pp. 89–90.
3. *Ibid.*, p. 169.
4. *Ibid.*, p. 143.
5. *Ibid.*, p. 141.
6. *Ibid.*, p. 53.
7. *Ibid.*, p. 139.
8. *Ibid.*, p. 145.
9. *Ibid.*, p. 80.
10. *Ibid.*, p .47.
11. *Ibid.*, p. 117.
12. *Ibid.*, pp. 152–3.

13. *Ibid.*, p. 80.
14. *Ibid.*, pp. 103–4.

18. 'MARY CRAWFORD': THE REINCARNATION OF ELIZA

1. Le Faye, *Jane Austen's 'Outlandish Cousin'*, pp. 129, 133.

19. EMMA

1. Letter from Jane Austen to Fanny Knight, 18/20 November 1814.

21. JANE AUSTEN: A LOSS OF YOUTH AND BLOOM

1. Caroline Austen, *My Aunt Jane Austen*, p. 5.
2. James E. Austen-Leigh, *A Memoir of Jane Austen*, p. 230.
3. David Cecil, *A Portrait of Jane Austen* (London: Penguin Books, 1980), p. 112.
4. Letter from Jane Austen to Cassandra Austen, 27/28 October 1798.
5. Letter from Jane Austen to Cassandra Austen, 24/26 December 1798.
6. Letter from Jane Austen to Cassandra Austen, 2 June 1799.
7. Letter from Jane Austen to Cassandra Austen, 25 January 1801.
8. Letter from Jane Austen to Cassandra Austen, 30 April 1811.
9. Letter from Jane Austen to Cassandra Austen, 5/8 March 1814.
10. Henry Austen, *Biographical Notice of the Author* (1818) in James E. Austen-Leigh, *A Memoir of Jane Austen*, p. 138.
11. Caroline Austen, *My Aunt Jane Austen*, p. 13.
12. Letter from Jane Austen to Cassandra Austen, 8/9 September 1816.
13. Letter from Jane Austen to James E. Austen, 16/17 December 1816.
14. Letter from Jane Austen to Alethea Bigg, 24 January 1817.
15. Letter from Jane Austen to Fanny Knight, 23/25 March 1817.
16. Caroline Austen, *My Aunt Jane Austen*, pp. 14–15.
17. Letter from Jane Austen to Charles Austen, 6 April 1817.
18. Letter from Jane Austen to Anne Sharp, 22 May 1817.
19. Letter from Jane Austen to James E. Austen, 27 May 1817.
20. James E. Austen-Leigh, *A Memoir of Jane Austen*, p. 130.
21. Letter from Jane Austen to Frances Tilson, 28/29 May 1817.

22. JANE'S MYSTERY ILLNESS EXPLAINED

1. Sir Zachary Cope, 'Jane Austen's Last Illness' in the *British Medical Journal*, 18 July 1964.
2. *Encyclopaedia Britannica*, 1911.
3. Dr Tony Smith, *Complete Family Health Encyclopaedia*.
4. Letter from Jane Austen to Cassandra Austen, 17/18 November 1798.
5. Letter from Jane Austen to Cassandra Austen, 12/13 May 1801.
6. Letter from Jane Austen to Cassandra Austen, 21/22 May 1801.
7. Helen and Gavin Turner Lefroy (eds), *The Letters of Mrs Lefroy* (Winchester: Sarsen Press, 2007), p. 35.
8. Le Faye, *Jane Austen's 'Outlandish Cousin'*, p. 160.
9. Letter from Jane Austen to Cassandra Austen, 3 November 1813.
10. Letter from Jane Austen to Cassandra Austen, 6/7 November 1813.
11. Caroline Austen, *My Aunt Jane Austen*, p. 11.
12. Letter from Jane Austen to Cassandra Austen, 17 October 1815.
13. James E. Austen-Leigh, *A Memoir of Jane Austen*, p. 91.
14. A.H.A. Asbroek, et al., 'Estimation of Serial Interval and Incubation Period of Tuberculosis using DNA Fingerprinting', in *The International Journal of Tuberculosis and Lung Disease*, Vol. 3, No. 5, May 1999. (Paris: International Union Against Tuberculosis and Lung Disease.)
15. Letter from Jane Austen to Cassandra Austen, 24/25 December 1798.
16. Letter from Jane Austen to Cassandra Austen, 2 June 1799.
17. Letter from Jane Austen to Cassandra Austen, 11 June 1799.
18. Letter from Jane Austen to Cassandra Austen, 19 June 1799.
19. *Ibid.*
20. Letter from Jane Austen to Cassandra Austen, 27/28 October 1798.
21. Letter from Jane Austen to Cassandra Austen, 1/2 December 1798.
22. Letter from Jane Austen to Cassandra Austen, 18/19 December 1798.
23. David Selwyn (ed), *The Complete Poems of James Austen* by James Austen, July 1814.
24. Deirdre Le Faye, *Reminiscences of Jane Austen's Niece Caroline Austen* (The Jane Austen Society, 2004), p. 45.
25. Jane Austen, *Love & Freindship and Other Writings* (London: Phoenix, 1998), p. 90.

24. THE DEATH OF JANE AUSTEN

1. Letter from Cassandra Austen to Fanny Knight, 20 July 1817.
2. Letter from Caroline Austen to James E. Austen-Leigh, 1869(?), National Portrait Gallery, RWC/HH, Folios 8–10, in James E. Austen-Leigh, *A Memoir of Jane Austen*, p. 187.
3. *Ibid.*
4. Letter from Cassandra Austen to Fanny Knight, 20 July 1817, in Deirdre Le Faye, *Jane Austen's Letters*, CEA/1.
5. Letter from Cassandra Austen to Fanny Knight, 29 July 1817.

25. EPILOGUE

1. Letter from Jane Austen to Cassandra, 27/28 December 1808.
2. Letter from Jane Austen to Fanny Knight, 30 November 1814.
3. Letter from Jane Austen to Fanny Knight, 13 March 1817.
4. Caroline Austen, *My Aunt Jane Austen*, pp. 2, 5, 10.
5. *Ibid.*, p. 6.
6. James E. Austen-Leigh, *A Memoir of Jane Austen*, p. 16.

Bibliography

Adams, Oscar Fay, *The Story of Jane Austen's Life*, USA: Chicago, 1891

Austen, Caroline, *My Aunt Jane Austen: A Memoir*, The Jane Austen Society, 1999

Austen, Jane, *Emma*, London: Penguin Books, 2003

———, *Persuasion*, London: Penguin Books, 2003

———, *Pride and Prejudice*, London: Penguin Books, 2003

———, *Mansfield Park*, London: Penguin Books, 2003

———, *Northanger Abbey*, London: Penguin Books, 2003

———, *Sense and Sensibility*, London: Penguin Books, 1969

———, *Love & Freindship and Other Writings*, London: Phoenix, 1998

———, *Lady Susan, The Watsons and Sanditon*, London: Penguin Books, 2003

Austen-Leigh, Emma, *Jane Austen and Lyme Regis*, London: Spottiswoode, Ballantyne and Co., 1946

Austen-Leigh, James E., *A Memoir of Jane Austen*, Oxford: Oxford University Press, 2002

Austen-Leigh, Mary Augusta, *Personal Aspects of Jane Austen*, Philadelphia: Pavilion Press, 2003

Austen-Leigh, William, *Jane Austen: Her Life and Letters – A Family Record*, London: Smith, Elder & Co., 1913

Brabourne, Lord Edward, *Letters of Jane Austen*, London: Richard Bentley & Son, 1884

Cecil, David, *A Portrait of Jane Austen*, London: Penguin Books, 1980

Chapman, R.W., *Jane Austen: Facts and Problems*, Oxford: Clarendon Press, 1948

——— (ed), *Jane Austen's Letters to her sister Cassandra and Others*, London: Oxford University Press, 1964

Evans, J.M., *Jane Austen: Northanger Abbey*, London: James Brodie

Henshaw, Henry (Agent to the Steventon Estate), *Steventon, Hampshire: Historical Notes and Anecdotes*, 1949

Hill, Constance, *Jane Austen: Her Homes and Her Friends*, London: John Lane, 1904

Le Faye, Deirdre, *Fanny Knight's Diaries*, The Jane Austen Society. 2000

——, *Jane Austen's 'Outlandish Cousin'*, London: The British Library, 2002

—— (collector and editor), *Jane Austen's Letters*, Oxford: Oxford University Press, 1997

——, *Jane Austen's Steventon*, Winchester: Sarsen Press, 2007

——, *Reminiscences of Jane Austen's Niece Caroline Austen*, The Jane Austen Society, 2004

Lefroy, Helen and Gavin Turner (eds), *The Letters of Mrs Lefroy*, Winchester: Sarsen Press, 2007

Matthew, H.C.G. and Harrison, Brian (eds), *Oxford Dictionary of National Biography*, Oxford: Oxford University Press, 2004

Nokes, David, *Jane Austen: A Life*, New York: Farrar, Straus and Giroux, 1997

Russell, P.M.G., *A History of the Exeter Hospitals, 1170–1948*, Exeter: Exeter Post-Graduate Medical Institute, 1976

Selwyn, David (ed), *The Complete Poems of James Austen* by James Austen, The Jane Austen Society, 2003

——, *Jane Austen: Collected Poems and Verse of the Austen Family*, Manchester: Carcarnet Press, 1996

Smith, Dr Tony, *Complete Family Health Encyclopaedia*, British Medical Association, London: Dorling Kindersley, 1990

Index